AQUASCAPING

AQUASCAPING

A STEP-BY-STEP GUIDE TO PLANTING, STYLING,

AND MAINTAINING BEAUTIFUL AQUARIUMS

GEORGE FARMER

CO-FOUNDER OF THE UK AQUATIC PLANT SOCIETY (UKAPS)

Skyhorse Publishing

Skyhorse Publishing books may be purchased in bulk at special discounts for sales promotion, corporate gifts, fund-raising, or educational purposes. Special editions can also be created to specifications. For details, contact the Special Sales Department, Skyhorse Publishing, 307 West 36th Street, 11th Floor, New York, NY 10018 or info@skyhorsepublishing.com.

Skyhorse® and Skyhorse Publishing® are registered trademarks of Skyhorse Publishing, Inc.®, a Delaware corporation.

Visit our website at www.skyhorsepublishing.com.

10 9 8 7 6 5 4 3 2

Library of Congress Cataloging-in-Publication Data is available on file.

Cover design by Brian Peterson
Cover photograph courtesy of the author

Print ISBN: 978-1-5107-5338-9
Ebook ISBN: 978-1-5107-5339-6

Printed in China

For Emma

CONTENTS

The author's 85-gallon aquascape in his home, photographed during the final stages of completing this book.

Aquascaping offers a unique way to connect with nature in any living space.

INTRODUCTION
WHAT IS AQUASCAPING?

Aquascaping is the art of creating beautiful aquariums. I like to explain the term as landscape gardening . . . but under water. It is well known that aquariums provide therapeutic value to those who view them for any length of time. They can help reduce levels of anxiety and induce a state of relaxation that is so important with today's often stressful modern living. As such, aquascaping allows us the ability to enjoy a unique connection with nature and all of the health benefits it provides.

Sitting in front of an aquarium is well-known to induce a state of relaxation.

The aquarium setting is not just limited to the home environment. They can be found in hospitals, medical waiting rooms, and rest homes, as well as busy offices and school reception areas. In my opinion, if an aquarium is decorated beautifully with natural materials such as live aquatic plants, wood, and rocks, then the therapeutic value is greatly enhanced.

The author's Oase StyleLine 85 aquarium is featured on the popular meditation app, Headspace.

The aim of this book is to show how *you* can create your own beautiful aquascape with live aquarium plants while enjoying the huge array of benefits this wonderful hobby and art form can provide. The principles can be applied to any form of aquarium, but the main focus of this book involves the use of aquarium plants with details on how you can make them thrive using modern techniques that I have had

The combination of water, wood and rocks, live plants, and fish creates a wonderful slice of nature.

success with for many years. No matter your experience level, by the end of this book you will have the knowledge to create your own beautiful slice of nature.

CONNECTING WITH NATURE

Aquascaping is different from any other art form because it is so rich and diverse. There is the design element where rocks, wood, and plants are positioned in a manner to provide a pleasing aesthetic balance and overall impression. The aquarium is a three-dimensional canvas where consideration needs to be given to where each component relates to one another across the length, height and depth of the layout. The nature of live plants means that they grow at different rates, obtaining different colors and textures that blend into one another as the aquascape matures. It is like a constantly evolving living sculpture that we have an element of control over as both the creator and the maintainer. I think it is this creation process combined with the regular maintenance that really gives us something very special to enjoy. Aquascaping provides a true connection with nature that is so important to experience in today's world where we are spending so much of our working and leisure time on digital devices and social media platforms that are constantly demanding our attention. Simply viewing our aquascape for any length of time helps to restore a sense of peace and the process of maintaining gives a real sense of achievement and element of control over something beautiful that we have had hand in creating. I also believe there is something deeply soothing about being close to water, as it provides a fundamental source of comfort and security. Along with the sense of movement, colors, light, and the living animals that are contained within this wonderful space, I believe an aquascape is the ultimate blend of art and nature that has the potential to enrich everyone's life. I am sure it can enrich yours too and my hope is that this book will start you on one of the most exciting, rewarding and relaxing journeys you have ever encountered. My dear friend, Balázs Farkas, co-founder of the world-famous aquascaping store, Green Aqua, says it best at the start of every YouTube video they create: "Welcome to the beautiful world of aquascaping!"

This aquascape gallery in Poland belonging to Adam Paszczela is a great source of inspiration and tranquility.

CHAPTER ONE
HOW TO GET STARTED

"A journey of a thousand miles begins with a single step."

—Laozi

Getting started in your aquascaping journey can be equally exciting and daunting, with a seemingly infinite variety of aquarium equipment, methodologies, and aquascaping styles to choose from. A quick Google or YouTube search can soon lead you to a plethora of well-intended but often conflicting advice from hobbyists of all experience levels, which is bound to lead to confusion. However, the great news is that there are many different ways to achieve success with your aquascapes suiting all levels of budget, skill, and spare time you have. You just have to choose the right path that helps you define and achieve your goals. The aim of this book is to simplify the entire process, providing you with the knowledge and confidence to get the right start, ultimately leading to the goal of being able to plan, create and maintain your own beautiful aquascapes.

WHY CHOOSE LIVE PLANTS?

Live aquarium plants offer numerous benefits to the entire aquarium ecosystem. Firstly, they look great—which is perfect for aquascaping, as the main goal is to create a beautiful piece of living art. Plants also produce

Live aquarium plants look beautiful, but also provide a wide range of biological benefits to the entire aquarium system.

oxygen and remove harmful nutrients from the tank's water, helping to ensure a healthy environment for all of the aquarium inhabitants, including fish, shrimp, snails, and beneficial bacteria. The plants also offer a sense of shelter and security to the fish, with many species relying on them in order to display breeding behavior. The growth of healthy aquarium plants helps prevent nuisance algae growth—the worst enemy of most aquarium keepers. By focusing on maintaining healthy plants in your aquarium, you can ensure a beautiful, thriving and algae-free aquascape that is guaranteed to provide you and your visitors with a sense of wonder and tranquility.

CHOOSING THE RIGHT AQUARIUM

This off-the-shelf aquarium is ideal for growing easy aquarium plant species.

Deciding on the right aquarium for you depends on several factors. How much are you willing to invest in terms of time, energy, and money? A small, low maintenance aquascape can cost less to buy initially and be much cheaper to set up and maintain in the long term.

This 12-inch cube aquarium is relatively low in cost to set up and maintain, and adds a positive impact to any living space.

A large, high-tech aquarium can be relatively expensive outlay with potentially much higher maintenance. It therefore follows that one of the most important decisions you need to make is fixing a budget and timetable, ensuring these are in line with your expectations. The good news is that you can create a beautiful living work of art without much expense or sacrificing too much time. The key to success is choosing the right aquarium, the right plants and decor, and the right livestock.

Jeff Senske from Aquarium Design Group showing how to match an aquarium effectively with interior design.

Aquariums come in all shapes, sizes, and even materials. The most common type is the rectangular glass aquarium, which can range in size from less than a gallon to several thousand. Acrylic aquariums are generally more expensive but are stronger, lighter, and have higher transparency. The main disadvantage is that they are easily scratched. Many aquariums come in a kit form, with supplied lighting, filtration, and heating, making them ideal for less experienced hobbyists.

Custom-built aquarium systems can be relatively expensive and complex to install but the rewards can be worthwhile.

The lighting will typically be suitable for easy plants and they remain a popular entry into aquascaping for many.

My first ever aquarium was a Juwel Rio 125 (33 gallons / 125 liters), and I enjoyed creating many successful aquascapes in this off-the-shelf system. I did eventually customize the lighting and added other equipment so I could grow more demanding plants, but to this day that aquarium remains one of my all-time favorites, having taught me so many lessons in aquascaping.

OFF-THE-SHELF VS. CUSTOM BUILT

A regular kit aquarium that's supplied with lighting, filtration, and a heater is most folks' entry into the hobby. They are typically very affordable and take a lot of guesswork and potential confusion out of having to choose

This Dennerle NanoCube aquarium kit comes supplied with the basics to help get you started on your aquascaping journey.

A high-end 125-gallon custom-built aquarium featuring slow growing and low maintenance plants make it ideal for a long-term aquascape.

circulation also costs less. Therefore, the key to success with creating a beautiful aquascape with these entry-level systems is to only use easier plants (we will go through a list of species that will likely succeed in the chapter on choosing your plants). Alternatively, you can opt to customize your aquarium by purchasing the individual components separately. This allows you to tailor the exact system to suit your requirements and potentially future-proof your system if and when you decide to try more challenging plant species and aquascapes. The range of aquariums, lighting, filters, heaters, and other hardware options can be bewildering for beginners, but the advice herein will steer you on the right path.

SIZE MATTERS

This tiny aquarium holds just 3 gallons and is home to tiny shrimp. Such small aquariums are not appropriate for most fish species.

the individual components yourself. The main issue with many of these kits is that they are often underpowered in terms of lighting and circulation for many plant species, because the manufacturers assume plastic plants and artificial decor will be used. Lower power lighting and

Deciding on which size of aquarium to own should depend on several factors. Practical considerations—such as cost and available space—are essential. However, there are biological factors at play, too: the

Staring in awe into the world's largest Nature Aquarium aquascape in Lisbon, Portugal. Created by the late Takashi Amano before he sadly passed in 2015.

larger the volume of water, the more environmentally stable the tank will be. For one, temperature and water chemistry fluctuations are lessened in larger aquariums. In addition, organic waste products created from the livestock—fish, shrimps, snails, and plants—are diluted further in larger volumes of water, and the diversity of stocking options are therefore increased.

Smaller aquariums—sometimes referred to as nano tanks—are quite popular, but their stocking levels in both quantity and size of the livestock are greatly reduced. Any waste produced has a higher chance for negative impact on water quality, with temperature and water chemistry fluctuations becoming more pronounced. Because nano tanks are generally much more affordable than their larger counterparts, they are more popular—especially with first-time owners. It is therefore essential that the owner does their research with particular attention being paid to the livestock's fully mature size. Typically, when many fish and plants are initially purchased, they are young specimens and have the potential to soon outgrow a smaller aquarium. The well-known statement, "the fish only grow to the size of their tank" is a myth, and although living quarters that are too small may stunt the animal's growth, it will surely outgrow the aquarium and cause suffering as a consequence. Remember: the animal's welfare should always be the primary consideration in any aquarium and aquascape environment. After all, these are living creatures and should be treated as such.

This popular Fluval Flex 15 gallon aquarium comes supplied with suitable lighting and filtration to be able to grow easy plants.

The easy to keep and breed cherry shrimp make an ideal stocking option for small aquariums.

HOODS OR RIMLESS?

Another major consideration is whether to opt for an aquarium with a hood or to go for a rimless tank. Most kit aquariums come with a hood that will often include the lighting built in, although it is also possible to remove an existing hood and customize with your own choice of lighting. Older style aquariums come with bracing bars and rims around the edges that house glass condensation panes. These bracing bars and rims add structural integrity to the main aquarium glass panels, allowing for the aquarium to be made from thinner glass, which typically saves on cost. These aquariums have other advantages in that they prevent a lot of aquarium water evaporation and maintain their heat more efficiently versus a rimless tank. Often, the hood is made from the same material and in the same style as the aquarium cabinet or stand, which can be a major deciding factor in purchasing, so the aquarium harmonizes with the overall interior design of the living space. Hood and cabinets are usually available in a variety of finishes to suit a wide range of traditional or contemporary interior spaces, from light wood to gloss black and everything in between. Solid wood is the best quality but much heavier and more expensive, with fiberboard woods being cheaper and lighter, but

The contemporary design of this Oase StyleLine 85 aquarium system suits modern living spaces with its white hood and cabinet.

Open topped rimless tanks with low-iron glass and glass filter pipes are a popular choice for aquascapers wishing to minimize the visual impact of aquarium equipment.

more prone to water ingress that can result in the wood warping or swelling over time.

Rimless tanks have become more commonplace with aquascapers over the last twenty years or so. The concept was popularized by the Japanese aquascaping product company Aqua Design Amano, and relies on having no hood, no braces or rims on top of the aquarium. The smallest, safest amount of clear silicone sealant is usually used (many hooded tanks have black seals joining the glass together) and the overall effect is to minimize the impact of the aquarium on the surrounding environment, so it almost looks invisible. Low-iron glass is typically used, which has higher clarity than regular float glass that's found in most aquariums, and this helps to enhance this minimalist look. Even the filter pipes are made from glass with clear hoses to prevent as much visual distraction

as possible. Suspended lighting units with discrete legs that rest on the aquarium glass or pendant lights that are hung from the ceiling or mounting arms provide illumination to these open-topped aquariums.

The whole effect is to create the illusion of a floating column of water where the aquascape can be viewed with as little distraction as possible from potentially ugly equipment. Cabinets or stands for rimless tanks usually have a more contemporary design. Matte black, grey, and white are popular—plus there are options for glass and stainless steel designs as well.

Rimless aquariums are very popular with many aquascapers because they allow the aquascape to be viewed from above. Many aquarium plants will happily grow from the water surface and protruding wood is often used to create an enhanced natural effect.

The popular Harlequin rasbora is a great choice that looks stunning when kept in large shoals.

This 2-gallon desktop aquarium can see significant evaporation due to its small size.

Disadvantages with this style of aquarium include having to deal with evaporation, more energy required to heat the aquarium water and potential escaping livestock. If you do decide to go down the rimless route it is important to choose livestock that are less likely to jump. I typically use a lot of tetras, barbs, and some species of rasbora. The risk is greatly reduced with densely planted aquariums where the sense of shelter and security is much higher versus a sparsely decorated tank. Floating plants are another great way to provide shelter and additional benefits to your tank, which we will discuss later.

A fine example of a high-energy aquascape originally aquascaped by Filipe Oliveira from Aquaflora for Aquarium Gardens.

HOW TO GROW PLANTS

Before we go into how to make a beautiful aquascape, it's important that we learn first how to grow healthy plants without nuisance algae. It's worth mentioning algae at this early stage because it is the number one reason folks give up on their aquariums. The good news is that algae is very preventable by providing well-maintained conditions with appropriate equipment that in turn helps promote healthy plant growth. Algae's arch enemy is healthy plant growth in combination with a well-maintained and equipped aquarium.

LOW AND HIGH-ENERGY SYSTEMS

Growing plants in an aquarium can be a complex topic, so I like to break it down using two main methodologies: high and low-energy. Other common terms that you may have heard include low- and high-tech, but I find these misleading as it's not the technology that should be considered. More relevant is the amount of energy we are both consuming and creating.

Low-Energy

As the name implies, a low-energy planted aquarium both uses and produces lower energy levels. Lower levels of lighting are employed, and it's the light that's the primary driving factor behind plant growth. So by only using low levels of light, the plants grow more slowly and therefore require less food, which we call nutrients. Nutrients need to be supplied via the substrate and/or liquid fertilizers, and in some cases carbon dioxide injection. These topics will be covered in detail later, as well as how to determine if your aquarium has low or high lighting levels. Plants that grow slowly create less organic waste, and less organic waste means less risk of algae. The risk of algae is also reduced because we are using lower lighting level.

With low light levels, we are restricted to growing less demanding plant species—this needs to be considered when you are initially planning your aquascape and what plants you are likely to succeed with. Low-energy systems can be ideal for beginners and those on a budget or with limited spare time available for maintenance. Typically, water changes are fewer/smaller versus a high-energy system, and with the slower plant growth the overall maintenance time is shorter.

High-Energy

A high-energy planted aquarium—or aquascape—is the opposite of the low-energy system: it uses and creates more energy. Typically, moderate to high levels of lighting are employed, and consequently the plant growth is faster. Remember, light is the main driving force behind plant growth. Faster growing plants require more nutrients to ensure they are kept well fed to avoid nutrient deficiencies. Symptoms of a starving plant include pale or yellowing leaves and the triggering of nuisance algae. It is thought that a suffering plant actually releases chemicals into the water that can induce an algae bloom. For this reason, it is important to ensure the plants are regularly dosed with an appropriate liquid fertilizer or at least have a nutrient-rich substrate (we will discuss these topics in more detail later).

Higher levels of light also mean that the plants' requirement for carbon increases. Carbon is the most important nutrient for plants and they receive most of their carbon source from carbon dioxide (CO_2). CO_2 injection systems are a very popular and effective way to add this carbon, and you will learn more about CO_2 injections later. Another consideration with a high-energy system is its requirement for higher levels of circulation. This is to help ensure that all of the plants have equal opportunity to access the CO_2 and nutrients in the water. You guessed it . . . more on circulation later in this book. The main advantage to a high-energy system is your potential to grow any species of plant you wish. Brighter lighting is often more visually stunning, but be aware that these systems tend to be much more expensive, with maintenance times and the risk of algae issues increasing directly proportionally to the amount of light you are employing.

CHAPTER TWO
LIGHTING

Lighting is arguably the most important topic in the world of aquascaping and planted aquariums. We need light so we can physically observe the aquarium and, as discussed, it is the primary factor behind plant growth. Most entry-level aquarium kits come supplied with a light unit that should be capable of growing easy category plants (see the appendix for a complete list of easy plants), which make for a great start for new aquascapers. For instance, the Fluval Flex 15 gal (57 L) comes fitted with an 11-watt LED that I have had a proven track record with. With more experience and confidence in successful plant growing you may wish to try more demanding species and will need to upgrade your lighting to something more powerful. The most experienced aquascapers often have their aquariums custom built, so the lighting needs to be retrofitted accordingly. A good example would be a 24-inch (60-centimeter) long aquarium fitted with a Twinstar 600S LED lamp. Lighting is a complex topic worthy of an entire book in itself, but I will cover the basics required so you can go about selecting the appropriate lighting solution for your own aquarium.

PHOTOSYNTHESIS AND BALANCE
Photosynthesis is the process of the plant converting light and CO_2 into new plant growth and oxygen. The more light and CO_2 we have, the more potential plant growth (and organic waste produced from the plant) we achieve. However, for the plant to remain healthy and free from algae, we also need to supply it with other nutrients via a liquid fertilizer and/or nutrient-rich substrate with appropriate circulation. Balancing these components (light, CO_2, nutrients, and circulation) in combination with maintaining your aquarium effectively is the key to ensuring healthy plant growth while minimizing algae issues.

LIGHTING TYPES
The most commonly available type of aquarium lighting at the time of this writing includes light emitting diodes (LED) and fluorescent lamps. Metal halide lamps are occasionally used, but are becoming increasingly phased out due to their relative inefficiency, short lifespan, and excessive heat production. LED are the most efficient and popular today, with literally hundreds of models available ranging in all shapes, sizes, power output, and color spectrums. High-output and compact T5 fluorescent lamps still remain popular but are becoming increasingly overtaken by LEDs. Indeed, LED units are being designed to replace old fluorescent tubes in aquariums, just like they are in domestic and industrial settings. As a (very) general rule of thumb: the average LED unit is approximately twice as efficient as its fluorescent counterpart, meaning that if you

originally had a 24-watt high-output T5 fluorescent lamp in your aquarium, you could potentially provide a similar light output for 12 watts of LED. Please bear in mind that different manufactures and models can vary.

LED lamps are the most popular form of aquarium lighting offering higher efficiency and controllability than fluorescent lamps.

LIGHT MEASUREMENTS

POWER

Your light unit will have a power rating in watts. This is how much electricity the lamp (or lamps) will be consuming. How much light is actually being produced will depend on the lamp's efficiency. How much light is physically reaching your plants will depend on a host of other factors, such as clarity of the water, height of the water column, and distance of light unit from the water surface. As you can see, there are a lot of variables so it is challenging to establish a fixed rule for recommending a specific lighting solution.

As a very approximate guideline, you will usually require around 1w of LED light per US gallon (4 liters) of aquarium water to grow most easy aquarium plants, providing all other growth conditions are adequate. For example, a typical 20-gal (80-L) aquarium will require 20 watts of LED light. Please note that the quality of the light, how far away it is from the water and plants, the aquarium water parameters, etc. will all have an influence in how much light is required.

PAR

Traditional PAR meters are relatively expensive but are a useful device to measure the available lighting inside an aquarium.

Photosynthetic active radiation (PAR) is a term used to describe how much light is available for the plants and other photosynthetic organisms to use, such as corals. This light is part of the electromagnetic spectrum and measures 400 to 700 nano meters (nm). Broadly speaking, this wavelength of light is also what is visible to the human eye.

There are devices known as PAR meters that can be used to measure the amount of PAR that's emitted from your aquarium lighting, including units with sensors designed to be used under water. These can be expensive—yet useful—if you wish to ensure your lighting is appropriate for the plants you wish to grow. One of the most affordable units is the Seneye Reef which also monitors your aquarium temperature, pH, and ammonia levels in real time via your computer or smartphone.

The Seneye Reef monitoring system is an affordable way to measure PAR and other important aquarium parameters.

Here is a PAR guide to ensure you have enough light for your chosen aquarium plants. The plants are split into three categories: easy, medium, and advanced, with examples of these species in the Chapter Eight, "Choosing, Preparing, and Maintaining Your Aquarium Plants."

PAR reading at substrate level (µmol m-2 s-1)
10–30 easy
30–60 medium
60+ advanced

Note that some species will be able to adapt beyond the readings here depending on whether CO_2 injection is being used, other nutrient levels and water chemistry.

COLOR TEMPERATURE AND SPECTRUM

The color temperature of a lamp is measured in Kelvin (K). Put simply, a lamp with a lower color temperature appears more orange/yellow, and a higher color temperature more blue. Most lamps have a K rating designed for freshwater aquariums, which have a color temperature between 3,000K and 10,000K, with 6,500K being very popular. This is a useful measurement to give an idea of how the lamp will look to our eyes. The spectral output of a lamp differs from the color temperature in that it is a more useful guide to predict how the plants may use the light. For example, plants require blue and red peaks in the light spectrum to photosynthesize (grow). However, if we have a lamp with only peaks in the red and blue then it would appear purple to our eyes and not be very visually appealing. Many lamps are, therefore, constructed to have a green peak in their spectral output too, and are therefore known as full spectrum. Although the plant uses little green light (it reflects it back to our eyes, making the green

Flat source lighting provides an even light and color rendition throughout the aquascape.

color visible to us), many lamps designed for aquascaping have a strong green peak to enhance the viewing experience of our aquarium. Thankfully, for us, aquatic plants are usually very adaptable to a wide range of spectrums due to their evolution in nature; sometimes growing in the shade and in deep water, other times growing in full unrestricted sunlight and out of water. As a general rule of thumb, as long as the light is visible to the human eye—approximately 400 to 700nm—then the plant can utilize it as PAR.

Flat Source vs. Point Source Lighting

The majority of artificial light units are designed to produce a relatively flat light across the aquarium footprint. This gives a uniform light that illuminates the aquarium's inhabitants in a balanced manner. Light levels may drop off a little toward the edges of the tank, as they are furthest away from the light source. Fluorescent lamp units and LEDs are spread in a linear fashion across a unit are example of flat-source lighting.

The Shimmer Effect

LED point source lighting is becoming more popular in aquascaping due to the more natural and dramatic effects it can provide. This light source emits from a much smaller area, which creates more intense shadowing and shimmering. Point source lighting is similar to the sun in this respect, as it is the ultimate point source light. It usually provides a less uniform spread of light across the aquarium, often with significant light intensity drop-off at the edges of the aquarium footprint. Point source lighting is particularly useful when wishing to create the most natural lighting effect

This Kessil LED's point source lighting creates a natural shimmer effect inside and outside the aquarium.

off-putting for others. My advice is to see this style of light in action prior to any potentially expensive purchase, as most point source LED brands tend to demand a higher price.

PHOTOPERIODS AND RAMPING

The photoperiod is the length of time that the plants are illuminated. Aquarium plants can adapt to a wide range of photoperiods, typically from as little as four hours to up to sixteen or more. In most situations, an eight-hour photoperiod is suitable, as much more tends to encourage algae growth and much less results in slow or unhealthy plant growth. I usually recommend keeping the photoperiod consistent day to day by using a plug-in-timer set to switch the aquarium lights on and off, according to when you will be most likely viewing the aquarium. For example, I have my aquarium lights come on at 2 p.m. and turn off at 10 p.m. Some light units have integrated features, which allow you to program the photoperiod, and even more advanced models may allow you to program the light intensity and adjust the spectrum. Having the light intensity ramp up and down is preferable if possible, as it is less likely to startle your fish and shrimp. If there is an adjustable spectrum option, then it's popular to combine a start-up and end-phase photoperiod with lower intensities and warmer color spectrum (more yellow/orange), with the mid-photoperiod being highest intensity and cooler color temperature (white/blue).

possible and is most prominent when used in combination with a lot of water surface movement, as any ripples in the water refract the water, resulting in an often-desirable shimmer effect. This shimmer effect is popular for many aquarium owners but can also be

PRO TIP: PLUG-IN TIMERS

To ensure a consistent photoperiod every day, a plug-in-timer is a great solution. I use cheap mechanical timers available from your local hardware store or online marketplace. Digital timers are more expensive but have the advantage of saving the programmed time in the event of a power cut. Smart devices are also becoming more commonplace, allowing you to program your photoperiod with your smartphone. Consider having the photoperiod during the time when you are most likely going to be viewing the aquascape.

SUNLIGHT

Sunlight reaching your aquarium is usually undesirable for any prolonged length of time, as its intense and uncontrollable nature can often trigger algae growth on the aquarium glass, plants and decor. Direct sunlight can also heat up your aquarium water considerably, being more pronounced the

PRO TIP: THE SIESTA METHOD

A break in a photoperiod is commonly referred to as a siesta. For example, you have a 10-hour photoperiod with a 2-hour break in the middle. For example, lights on at 8 a.m., off at 2 p.m., then on again at 4 p.m. and off at 8 p.m. This has been attributed with helping to reduce the risk of algae but, at least in my experience, plants respond better to a consistent photoperiod. Algae is usually a sign of poor plant health and/or lack of aquarium maintenance, so it is always better to focus on fixing this rather than using a siesta. I run all of my planted aquarium for 8-straight hours.

smaller your aquarium. It is therefore very important to consider the location of your aquarium—especially during summer months. The exception to this where some hobbyists actually rely on the sunlight as

Our home aquarium receives some direct sunlight during summer months.

their main source of light to grow their plants but this should be done with caution—especially if fish and shrimp are present with considerable fluctuations in water temperature being a potential hazard to their health and well-being. If your aquarium receives some direct sunlight, then ensure your plants are fed with enough liquid fertilizer and CO_2 to cope with the extra light.

PEARLING

Many hobbyists like to see pearling in their planted aquariums. Pearling is witnessed as visible oxygen bubbles forming on plant leaves. This occurs when the plants are photosynthesizing at such a high rate that the aquarium water becomes saturated with oxygen. As the plants produce more oxygen, it forms bubbles on the leaves that often shoot to the aquarium surface. Pearling is usually only achieved in a higher energy system with higher lighting levels in combination with

CO_2 injection and other ideal nutrient levels. It's particularly noticeable if the filter is turned off, so the lack of circulation allows the oxygen bubbles to form more readily.

Fast-growing plants, such as this *Hydrocotyle tripartita*, produce more oxygen than slower growing species.

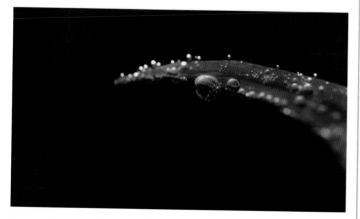

Beautiful oxygen bubbles forming on this *Cryptocoryne* leaf, known as "pearling."

CHAPTER THREE
FILTRATION, CIRCULATION, AND HEATING

The vast majority of aquariums require some form of filtration and circulation. There are of course exceptions, as some prefer to employ a filterless system—but these go beyond the scope of this book. Aquarium filters keep the aquarium water clean by mechanical, biological and sometimes chemical means. There are two main types of filter models: external and internal, each with their pros and cons, which we will discuss later in the book. What they do have in common is that they are largely responsible for simultaneously cleaning and circulating the aquarium water. Circulation is a critical element to keeping a healthy planted aquarium and aquascape, which will also be discussed in more detail later.

MECHANICAL FILTRATION

Mechanical filtration is the most basic form of filtering your aquarium water. It relies on passing water through some form of material that blocks waste debris and allows the cleaned water to return back to the aquarium. There are various materials that can be used for this, and most come supplied with any purchased filter. Filter floss is sometimes used, which can trap the finest of particles and is often employed as a temporary measure to really polish the water. The disadvantage of floss is that it does clog very quickly and requires more frequent cleaning. Sponges are popular, as they are inexpensive and easy to clean.

Different pore sizes trap different size particles with the finest sponges polishing the water most effectively, but conversely being the quickest to clog and therefore requiring the most frequent maintenance. Larger pore size sponges clog less quickly but will not trap so much debris. Cleaning mechanical filters should be done as frequently as necessary. This ensures an efficient flow and avoids an excess accumulation of organic waste and buildup of oxygen-consuming bacteria that can

Sponges are a popular form of filter media that can clean the water mechanically, biologically, and chemically.

trigger nuisance algae growth. The more efficient the water is flowing through the filter, the more oxygen can feed the filter bacteria. Note that mechanical filtration can also act as biological and chemical filtration, which we will cover next.

BIOLOGICAL FILTRATION

Biological filtration is a hugely important topic in the world of aquarium keeping. It is responsible for converting highly toxic waste products from the aquarium inhabitants into relatively harmless compounds. This process is known as the nitrogen cycle and begins with your livestock constantly excreting waste into the aquarium water. This waste results in a buildup of highly toxic ammonia and/or ammonium. Left

PRO TIP: TANK CYCLING

The traditional method of establishing beneficial bacteria in your new aquarium by using ammonia products or hardy fish is not necessary in a planted aquarium with plenty of healthy plants. The plant growth itself ensure any toxic ammonia/ammonium and nitrite is used before it can become harmful. For this reason, I like to densely plant my new aquarium with at least 25 percent fast-growing plants such as stems and floating species (see appendix for full plant species list). Their rapid nitrogen uptake allows for the stocking of your fish without the risk of "New Tank Syndrome," a common cause of fish fatality caused by excess ammonia and nitrite in non-planted aquariums.

unchecked, this will build and poison your livestock, resulting in their death, a phenomenon known as "New Tank Syndrome."

Thankfully, there are helpful bacteria that will feed on ammonia. These bacteria then produce another slightly less toxic waste product, resulting in nitrite. Finally, there is another form of bacteria that feeds upon this nitrite, resulting in the final waste product known as nitrate. Nitrate is relatively harmless, and it's this constant cycling of ammonia to nitrite to nitrate via the bacteria in our filters and substrates that allow us to keep fish, shrimp, and snails in a closed aquarium environment. Water changes are usually employed to dilute the buildup of nitrate. If the water changes are not large or frequent enough, then the nitrate will gradually build up over a period of several months. Left unchecked, the fish will often adapt to these high levels, but the addition of any new livestock can result in toxic shock, as the new fish have not adapted to these high nitrate levels. This is known as "Old Tank Syndrome."

Another very important factor to consider is plant growth. Plants require nitrogen as one of their main nutrients, with ammonia, nitrite, and nitrate all being nitrogen compounds and therefore acting as an essential food source for our plants. By promoting healthy plant growth, we can therefore significantly boost the biological filtration capacity of our aquarium. Plants also produce extra oxygen via photosynthesis, which also boosts the efficiency of the nitrifying bacteria. This is one of the many reasons I personally love to keep plants with any fish, if possible. It is important to note that more fish should not be added to deliberately increase nitrogen levels. This will simply place more demands on the filter and result in more organic waste accumulation, which will lead to water quality issues and potential algae problems. One of algae's biggest triggers is ammonia, and even a tiny spike can trigger an algae bloom.

BIOLOGICAL MEDIA

There are literally hundreds of different biological media types available for your filter. Most filters come supplied with sufficient media in the form of sponges (that also act as a mechanical filter) and/or ceramic or molded plastic pieces. These have a large surface area that allows for the colonization of nitrifying bacteria. It can be popular to replace the manufacturer's supplied biological media with an arguably more efficient third-party media. I tend to stick with the supplied media, comfortable knowing that my plant growth provides much of the required biological filtration.

CHEMICAL FILTRATION

Chemical filtration relies on a special filter media that uptakes a range of chemicals from the aquarium water depending on the media type. Activated carbon is the most popular and will adsorb a wide range of pollutants from the water; it's particularly useful for polishing the water and removing staining that can occur from any tannin leeching wood. It can also remove heavy metals and organic matter.

There is debate as to whether carbon filtration should be used in conjunction with liquid fertilizer, as it could potentially remove some of the useful plant nutrients. I like to use carbon or other chemical filtration as a temporary measure when wishing to achieve crystal-clear water for a photo shoot or video production. Other popular chemical medias include zeolite (for ammonia removal) and nitrate and phosphate removal resins. I tend to avoid these in planted aquariums as the plants are actually effective at using these compounds as a food source. A product from Seachem called Purigen is popular and is very effective at removing any staining from the water. It's advantage over activated carbon is that it can be re-charged once expired by using a bleach solution followed by an appropriate dechlorinator. The lifespans of all chemical medias are dependent on several factors, but you can expect most to last a few weeks with regular use. There is a lot of discussion about the removal of helpful nutrients from liquid fertilizers from activated carbon, but its affect is negligible. The use of both carbon filtration and regular dosing of liquid fertilizers works very well together without causing any detriment to plant growth.

INTERNAL FILTERS

Internal filters sit inside the aquarium. They have a relatively small filter media capacity but can have relatively high flow rates. These types of filters often rely on sponges to provide both mechanical and biological filtration, with some models offering carbon sponges or carbon-filled cartridges. These are often the cheapest type of filters and are particularly useful for smaller

This internal filter is disguised in the corner of the aquarium behind tall *Vallisneria* plants.

aquariums. My main issue with internal filters is their aesthetic impact in the aquarium and aquascape, as they are visually distracting unless disguised or hidden somehow.

The Oase BioPlus Thermo internal filter has the advantage of having a in-built and removable heater.

Most importantly, they also use up valuable space in the aquarium. Some models such as the Oase BioPlus Thermo do come with an integrated heater, which is a good design feature to help minimize the otherwise distracting view of a standalone heater. Some aquarium kits are fitted with a false background that houses the filtration system and compartment for a heater.

EXTERNAL FILTERS

External filters are situated outside the aquarium, often sited inside the aquarium cabinet or stand. They offer a much larger capacity for filter media, usually utilizing numerous baskets that can be fitted with a multitude of media types. They rely on having an inlet and outlet hose, where the water is drawn in through the inlet, where it then passes through the filter unit, then finally

External filters have many advantages over internal filters, including more media capacity and not impacting so aesthetically on the aquascape.

Glass filter inlets and outlets are popular with aquascapers with open-topped aquariums.

through the outlet. External filters are the best choice for aquascapes, as they present little visual distraction to the aquarium. Clear hoses and even glass inlets and outlets are often used to make their aesthetic impact almost invisible.

Stainless steel filter inlets and outlets are also available for a more modern look. These usually have to be purchased separately, with most external filters being supplied with black, gray, or green plastic fittings and hoses (which will usually spoil the view). One exception is the use of black filter fittings in conjunction with a black background in the aquarium, rendering it almost invisible. Some models of external filter come with integrated heaters such as some Eheim and Oase models. These hide an otherwise unsightly heater from view but also provide a more even heat distribution for the aquarium water.[1]

---

1   The Eheim models have an element fitted to the base of the filter, whereas the Oase models have a regularly styled removable heater that slots into the filter unit.

Hang-On-Back (HOB) Filters

These filters are very popular in the USA and have the advantage of taking up little space inside the aquarium. They are relatively inexpensive when compared with an external canister filer but have the disadvantage of providing less efficient circulation. This is due to their water return design that cascades downwards into the aquarium water rather than across the water column. For many aquascapes, having a box attached to the external part of the aquarium can also be visually distracting.

PRO TIP: FILTER MAINTENANCE

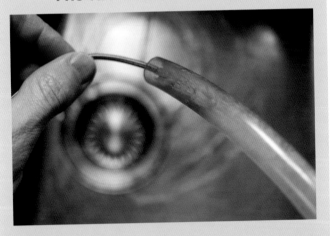

If you are performing a large water change, then use the time while the aquarium is being filled or emptied to clean your filter to maximize your aquarium maintenance efficacy!

Filters require regular maintenance for two main reasons: to keep them working efficiently in order to effectively perform biological filtration and to help maintain ideal circulation in the aquarium. Biological media shouldn't be excessively cleaned, otherwise the population of beneficial bacteria can be compromised. For this reason, any biological media should be cleaned in old aquarium water and not fresh tap water, as any chlorine can kill the beneficial bacteria. In order to maintain circulation levels, the filter pipes, hoses and impeller will need regular cleaning.

Any mechanical media can be thoroughly cleaned in running tap water or simply replaced with new media in the case of filter floss (often used as a pre-filter or to polish the water). Chemical media should be replaced or re-charged in accordance with the manufacturer's instructions.

SUMPS

Some large aquariums can be fitted with a sump that houses the aquarium filtration and other equipment. The sump is like a smaller aquarium, which usually sits below the main display aquarium in the cabinet. It's plumbed into the main display with hoses and/or ridged pipes and has the capacity to hold a lot more filter media, as well as separate heaters and any additional equipment you may wish to keep out of the main display. Setting up a sump usually requires a little more specialist knowledge, but they can be much more efficient and make them an easier to maintain filtration solution for large aquariums.

CIRCULATION

Circulation of the aquarium water is necessary to allow for improved oxygen exchange between the water column and the air above. Fish, shrimp, snails, and most filter bacteria have a constant demand on oxygen. The plants also require oxygen, as well as producing it via photosynthesis during lighting periods and then demand more oxygen at night where they respire by consuming oxygen and producing CO_2. Circulation is also important to allow for nutrients (especially CO_2 if used via a CO_2 injection kit . . . more on this later) to reach all of the aquarium plants. The higher energy your planted aquarium system (the more light it has, for instance), the more circulation you usually require. This is to ensure all of the plants have an equal opportunity to use the nutrients in the water. Higher levels of circulation are also useful to assist with mechanical filtration, as any debris and waste particles are more likely to be removed. If this waste is allowed to accumulate to excess on the plant leaves and/or substrate, this may eventually lead to poor water quality and algae issues.

METHODS OF CIRCULATION

Circulation is most often provided by the aquarium filter but can also be further assisted by internal pumps—often known as powerheads—which fit inside the aquarium and simple pump water in any given direction. A common technique for larger aquariums is to supplement the use of an external filter with an additional powerhead. This is especially useful if you are on

PRO TIP: POWERHEADS

Powerheads are small water pumps that are fitted inside the aquarium that produce extra flow and circulation. They are an inexpensive way to boost your overall aquarium circulation and can be easily hidden from view. Attention should be paid to ensure no livestock can enter the inlet part of the pump, although most are fitted with a strainer guard. The direction of the pump's flow should be considered to give the best overall circulation pattern in the aquarium without excessively disturbing the plants.

Some powerheads offer an adjustment nozzle so you can adjust the flow output to best suit your aquarium. Other types are designed to give a more widespread flow pattern, which can be helpful for avoiding too much turbulence. Often it is a case of trial and error until you find a solution that works for your particular system.

a budget, with powerheads being less expensive than an additional filter. You could also use combinations of internal and external filters if required to improve overall filtration and circulation capacity.

Turnover

Aquarium water turnover is a useful way to measure overall circulation rate. It's usually measured by looking at the filter's flow rate and calculating the aquarium's total volume being pumped per hour. For example, a 20-gal (80-L) aquarium fitted with a 100 gallons per hour (400 liters per hour) filter gives us an ideal turnover. Sometimes more is necessary with very high-energy systems and often less can be managed effectively. There are many variables to determining what circulation levels are ideal, with some trial and error often being necessary to get the best results.

Filter Outlets

The design on the filter outlet component can have a huge impact on the circulation pattern produced in an aquarium. There are various filter outlet designs, from a straightforward nozzle to spray bars and lily pipes. Each have their own pros and cons, and their use should be considered depending on the size and style of aquarium. The overall aim for most planted aquariums is to achieve a level of circulation where all of the plants are gently moving with water movement. Try to avoid situations with excess turbulence where some plants may be getting physically impaired by too much flow. Lily pipes and spray bars are useful for helping to circulate the water effectively. My preference, in most situations, are glass lily pipes due to their combination of subtle aesthetic impact and design. The lily shaped outlet helps to move the water well through the aquarium while simultaneously creating a small amount of surface movement, which helps to improve oxygen exchange. The main disadvantage to glass pipes are their fragility and they must be cleaned frequently in order to prevent an unsightly build-up of organic waste and algae.

FILTER INLETS AND SKIMMERS

The filter inlet on internal filters is built into the unit, but there are various options available when using an external filter. Most external filters are supplied with a basic plastic U-bend fitting; one end connected to the filter hose and the other going into the aquarium. This has a fitting on the end, with strainer slots to allow for aquarium water in-flow. The strainer slots prevent the accidental suction of livestock and large debris. One possible upgrade is to use a glass or stainless steel inlet, which also doubles up as an aquarium water surface skimmer. This has a floating portion that water is drawn through at the same time as water is flowing through the inlet strainers. A common issue with many planted aquariums is the accumulation of a floating organic film (surface scum), so this skimming action is ideal. There are also separately powered devices that skim the water surface, with a very popular model being the Eheim Skim 350.

HEATING THE AQUARIUM WATER

The water temperature required for most planted aquariums and aquascapes is between 68°F/20°C to 82°F/28°C. There are exceptions to this range, and appropriate research should be carried out before owning any fish. Aquarium plants are adaptable to a large range of temperatures, so do not be concerned with this. It is worth noting that the rate of all biological processes in the aquarium are determined by the temperature of the water. The higher the temperature, the quicker your fish will breathe and create waste, and the more food they will require. Plants will grow more quickly, demand more nutrients, and create more waste at such temperatures. Algae will have the potential to grow more rapidly. Aquarium water also carries less oxygen in warmer water. For this reason, I like to keep my aquarium water at the cooler end of what my chosen fish are comfortable with, and recommend you do the same to reduce maintenance times and the risk of algae.

HEATER TYPES

There are two main types of heaters available: internal and external. They both contain a heating element and usually a built-in thermostat to maintain a consistent temperature. The advantage of internal heaters is that they are usually much less expensive than external models and do not require an external filter to operate. Disadvantages are that they tend to look unsightly and can spoil the aesthetic of an aquascape (unless hidden). The position of an internal heater also needs to be considered so that it has a flow of water around it to ensure

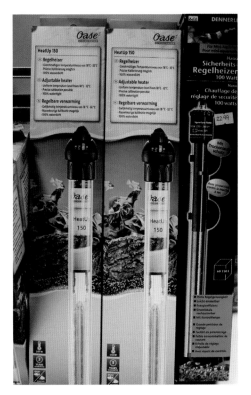

The power of the heater needs to match the size and ambient temperature of the aquarium.

even heating of the aquarium water. External heaters are fitted to an external filter on the outlet side so that the flowing water is heated, ensuring an evenly heated aquarium. They are usually more expensive than their internal counterparts and can potentially restrict some flow from the filter due to their fitment to the external filter hose. External heaters also require cleaning on their internal surfaces in order to avoid a buildup of organic waste from restricting flow. I recommend this is carried out at the same time as cleaning the external filter hose; usually every two to four weeks to ensure flow efficiency.

CHAPTER FOUR
FEEDING AQUARIUM PLANTS

Plants require food—known as nutrients—in order to grow. Plants can receive nutrients from both their roots and their leaves. A nutrient-rich substrate provides food to the plant roots, and liquid fertilizers provide nutrients to the plant leaves through the aquarium water (water column). Ideally, we should add nutrients via both the substrate and water column in order for plants to thrive as much as possible. The healthier the plant, the more ability it has to fight off potential algae. If a plant goes too hungry—known as nutrient deficiency—it exhibits poor growth, pale leaves, or leaves with holes that can trigger algae growth. First signs usually appear on the weakest leaves. For this reason, it is very important to consider an appropriate nutrient dosing regimen to help keep the plants as healthy as possible.

SUBSTRATES

The substrate is the bottom layer in the aquarium and serves a variety of purposes. Mainly, it provides a physical anchor for the plant roots to prevent them from floating. A substrate will often contain nutrients in order to feed the plant roots, as well as providing a home for beneficial bacteria that can assist with biological filtration and the breakdown of organic waste. Substrates can also assist with the aesthetic impact of the aquascape. For example, the use of cosmetic sand is popular where no plants are added. These sands are often used in the foreground instead of using foreground plants, or as pathways to give a great sense of depth to an aquascape. Substrates should also be chosen with consideration given to the livestock. Some fish species have sensitive barbels (similar to whiskers) that can potentially be damaged on a substrate with sharp edges. Some fish also like to bury themselves, and so may not be the ideal candidate for a densely planted aquarium with delicate roots.

INERT GRAVEL AND SAND

The most basic form of substrate is an inert gravel of sand. This contains no nutrients but is the cheapest and most commonly available, with a huge variety of colors,

Regular dosing of liquid fertilizers are required to feed the plants through their leaves.

Decorative or cosmetic sand isn't ideal for plant growth but perfect for its aesthetic value.

Adding larger grains of gravel to the sand adds a natural feel to the aquascape foreground.

grain sizes, and textures. These are great in a purely cosmetic role when used to give an open foreground or pathway effect, as discussed earlier. An aquarium with an inert substrate is capable of growing healthy plants, but an emphasis needs to be placed on a high quantity of appropriate dosing of liquid fertilizers in order for the plants to receive sufficient nutrients. The size of the gravel or sand grains needs to be considered. Larger gravels over 5 mm in grain size are usually unsuitable due to their restriction on allowing root penetration for plants with more delicate roots. In contrast, fine sands can present an issue in the longer term with them compacting and also preventing root penetration. Another risk for fine sand—especially if deeper layers are added—is an area underneath where no oxygen is present. This can lead to the excess production of anaerobic bacteria and ultimately poisonous and foul-smelling hydrogen sulfide gas. I usually recommend a grain size of between 1 mm and 3 mm for inert gravels and sands. Your chosen color should depend on your taste and the overall aesthetic impact you desire.

NUTRIENT-RICH BASE LAYER

A nutrient-rich base layer is a way to add nutrients to the substrate while still using an inert gravel or sand. Keep in mind that it needs to be added to the bottom the aquarium before your gravel or sand. There are varieties of suitable products available, including Tropica Plant Substrate. Some hobbyists like to use a garden soil or compost as their base layer. The results can be effective, but as it is not a controlled product there is a risk of excess organics, including toxic ammonia, leeching in the aquarium water, so exercise caution if you decide to take this route. A product that many have good experience with is Miracle-Gro Organic Potting Soil or John Innes No.3 Compost.

ROOT CAPSULES

Nutrition Capsules are perfect for target-feeding specific plants at their roots.

Aquarium Soil is a great all-in-one substrate designed to feed the plants through their roots and can also soften the aquarium water.

Root capsules or tablets are an inexpensive and simple way to add more nutrients to any existing substrate. They can be used to target feed specific plants or added en masse during the setup process to provide nutrients to the entire substrate footprint. There are many brands available, but I would recommend one that contains the widest range of nutrients possible. They need to be buried sufficiently under the substrate surface to prevent any excess nutrients leeching into the water column and so should be done before adding water to the aquarium.

AQUARIUM SOILS

My favorite substrate is a complete aquarium soil. There are many brands available with the majority being derived from a naturally occurring soil material—often volcanic ash–based—which has been prepared by pelletizing and baking. Most soils are rich in nutrients with a structure making them suitable for root penetration and bacteria colonization. These soils will often reduce the hardness of the water and reduce the pH slightly, which most aquarium plants and tropical fish prefer. Unlike most gravels and sands, they should not be prerinsed or washed, making their installation quick and easy. Most soils are designed to be used on their own with no need for a nutrient-rich base layer. The exception is the ADA substrate system that recommends the use of several different substrate products—as well as a soil—making it relatively expensive but providing excellent results.

One of the great characteristics of soils is their ability to take in nutrients from the water column and release them back to the plants through their roots. This combined with the nutrients already present in the soil and the addition of liquid fertilizers help to ensure that the plants are well fed at all times. Typical grain sizes for most brands of soil are between 2–5 mm, with some brands also offering powder varieties that have a smaller grains of around 1 mm. These are ideal for plants with fine and delicate roots, such as many foreground carpeting species, such as *Hemianthus callitrchoides* "Cuba" and *Glossostigma elatinoides*. Some soil products are known to leech high levels of toxic ammonia during the initial start-up phase of the aquarium process.

During this phase, it is essential to perform large, frequent water changes and avoid the addition of any livestock. The testing for ammonia and nitrite is a good idea to ensure that adding livestock is safe. The good news is that this ammonia will help to seed your filtration system with beneficial nitrifying bacteria.

Some Aquarium Soil brands are available in small or regular grain sizes ranging from under 1 mm to 5 mm.

Most soils have porous structures for ideal bacteria colonization, and the soil's low density allow for unrestricted root penetration. After several months, most soils will begin to degrade and lose their structure, eventually turning into a mud-like substance. This should not cause issue unless you are keeping fish that like to dig (which I would personally avoid in most planted aquariums) or you intend to often move decor and plants around the aquarium. This will result in cloudy water, and the disturbance of the soil can potentially leech excess nutrients into the water column that may trigger algae. If you do end up disturbing any substrate excessively, then a pro tip is to immediately perform a large water change (at least 50 percent) to help prevent an algae bloom.

Aquarium soils are more expensive than inert gravels and/or sands with a nutrient-rich base layer, but their advantages make the extra investment worthwhile in most circumstances.

SUBSTRATE DEPTH

There is no real optimum substrate depth, but some guidelines should definitely be considered. Mainly, the substrate should be deep enough to allow for complete coverage for a majority of plant species. Exceptions include epiphyte plants that attach to the decor and have their roots exposed to the water column, and bulb plants that usually do best with the uppermost tip of the bulb just exposed above the substrate. Typically, a depth of at least 1 in (25 mm) is recommended for most situations. It is a common technique to have the substrate sloping upward, toward the rear of the aquarium. For example, a depth of 1.5 in (40 mm) at the front leading up to a depth of 4 in (100 mm) at the rear. From an aesthetic perspective, this gives the optical illusion that the aquarium appears deeper—front to back—than it actually is. It can also be useful if you are planning to use plant species with a large root structure in the background, as these will benefit from the larger nutrient content available to them (if using soil). Be careful not to go too deep with substrate that are not planted into, as the lack of oxygen can lead to the potential hydrogen sulfide issues previously mentioned. The good news is that you can have a soil layered as deep as required if it's planted. The roots produce oxygen that should help avoid the production of excess anaerobic bacteria. When aquascaping your aquarium, you can get creative with your substrate depth in order to give the best visual impact.

LIQUID FERTILIZERS

Plants have the ability to uptake nutrients through their leaves, and these nutrients are best supplied through liquid fertilizers added directly to the aquarium water. The topic of which product(s) to use and which method to dose liquid fertilizers is a hotly debated topic. I will begin by saying that the techniques I advocate are a result of many years of experience with planted aquariums using a wide variety of products and methodologies.

Aim for a liquid fertilizer that provides a comprehensive range of macro and micronutrients.

MACRO AND MICRONUTRIENTS

Nutrients come in two main forms: macro and micronutrients. Macros are what plants require in larger amounts and micros in much smaller quantities. The most important macronutrient of all is carbon. This is usually provided via small levels of carbon dioxide (CO_2) gas naturally present in the aquarium water and as a consequence of respiration from livestock and bacteria. We can add more CO_2 gas via an injection kit, which we will discuss in the next chapter. There are no liquid fertilizers at the time of this writing that will directly provide a meaningful level of extra carbon. That said, beware of products branded as "liquid CO_2" or "liquid carbon," as the active ingredient in these is a biocide called *glutaraldehyde*. Glutaraldehyde provides no real additional levels of carbon to plants and can be extremely toxic if overdosed. Although it can be used as an algaecide, I do not endorse its use as the risk outweighs any potential long-term reward. Other important macronutrients include nitrogen, phosphorus, and potassium—collectively referred to as NPK. Many liquid fertilizers do not include these nutrients because the belief was that nitrogen and phosphorous (nitrates and phosphates) would cause algae issues. We now know that these nutrients do *not* cause algae in healthy planted aquarium systems, but rather help to enhance plant growth and health. In fact, in many high-energy planted aquariums, the addition of nitrate and phosphates is essential to ensure the plants do not suffer from nutrient deficiencies, which will in turn lead to unhealthy plants and algae.

ESTIMATIVE INDEX

The Estimative Index (EI) is a popular nutrient dosing method to ensure your plants never go hungry. Another advantage to this method is that there will no longer be a need to test the aquarium water for nutrients. Macro and micronutrients are dosed daily, often via a DIY dry chemical solution, and a large quantity (usually 50 percent or higher) of aquarium water is changed weekly to ensure nutrient levels do not build to unsafe levels. Another very important function of the water change is to dilute the waste organics that have built up over the week from the livestock, plants, and bacteria. (We will cover the importance of water changes and the techniques used later.) There are many variations of the EI method that can be applied to almost any planted aquarium—whether it's low-energy or high-energy—but the same principle remains. I deliberately slightly overdose nutrients every day to ensure zero deficiencies and change a lot of water to reset these nutrient levels. I recommend visiting the Barr Report website for more information on EI dosing. (See the appendix for recommended URL links.)

ALL-IN-ONE LIQUID FERTILIZERS

My favorite method for adding nutrients to aquarium water is to use an all-in-one comprehensive liquid fertilizer, with the EI principle of daily dosing and large weekly water changes. I've used this method for many years now with all of my own aquascapes and for most of my clients', too. Many brands available include all the necessary nutrients in an ideal ratio and in one handy bottle. The idea is to dose the liquid fertilizer every day with the amount depending on the size and energy level of the aquarium. For example, a low-energy and small planted aquarium will require far less fertilizer than a large high-energy system. I developed a simple dosing method that works for most all-in-one fertilizers for most situations.

Low-energy (no CO_2 injection, low-moderate lighting, less plants)
1 ml per 10 gal (40 L) aquarium water per day
Medium energy (CO_2 injection, moderate lighting, more plants)
2 ml per 10 gal (40 L) aquarium water per day
High-energy (CO_2 injection, high lighting, high plant density)
5 ml per 10 gal (40 L) aquarium water per day

The above recommendation may differ from the manufacturer's recommendation, which usually underdose (in my experience). Most brands recommend just a weekly addition of liquid fertilizer, which I do not recommend due to the "feast or famine" nature of one large feed followed by potential nutrient starvation later in the week. It is also important to note that the use of a nutrient-rich substrate and soil can result in you not needing as much fertilizer, or if your tap water supply contains high levels of nutrients. The good news is that plants are able to use up excess nutrients through a phenomenon known as "luxury update," so even if you are overdosing and have sufficiently healthy plants, then this is not an issue. A slight excess of nutrients in a healthy planted aquarium are favorable to nutrient deficiencies, which can lead to unhealthy plants and algae.

Our 85-gallon aquascape is dosed with 30 ml of Tropica Specialised Nutrition every day.

The liverwort, *Riccardia chamedryfolia*, producing visible oxygen bubbles through photosynthesis.

Rotala 'Vietnam H'ra' requires strong lighting and CO_2 injection to get the best results.

CHAPTER FIVE
THE IMPORTANCE OF CARBON DIOXIDE

After light, carbon dioxide (CO_2) is the most important factor for plant growth. It is a fundamental part of the photosynthesis process, where plants use light and CO_2 to create new growth and oxygen. The opposite occurs in the evening through respiration, where the plant uses oxygen and creates CO_2. Around 40 percent of an aquarium plant is made from carbon, and for a plant to grow it needs more carbon. The best source of carbon is via CO_2 gas in the aquarium water. There is a low level of naturally occurring CO_2 in the aquarium that the plant uses, but to improve growth considerably and enable growth of a wider variety of plant species, we need to add more CO_2 via some form of injection. I recommend CO_2 injection for most planted aquarium owners and aquascapers, as you are guaranteed to have a much higher chance of success with your plants. However, CO_2 injection is not essential, with many successful aquascapes thriving without it. It can be a relatively expensive investment, and the use of pressurized CO_2 cylinders and CO_2 gas in general aren't without their risks (which will be discussed). The biggest disadvantage with non-CO_2 injection is the relatively slow plant growth and restriction of species that will thrive, therefore limiting your options for plant choice. You can see

CO_2 injection isn't necessary when using easy plant species, but will improve the growth of all aquarium plants.

a list of suitable plant species in the appendix, under the "Easy" category.

PRESSURIZED CO2 INJECTION KIT
The most popular, controllable, and reliable way to add more CO_2 gas into your planted aquarium is to invest in a pressurized CO_2 injection kit. They usually comprise of eight components that all work together to enable the safe delivery of CO_2 gas into the aquarium water.

A complete pressurized CO_2 system hooked up to an external filter is one of the most efficient ways to inject carbon dioxide.

Pressurized Cylinder

The pressurized cylinder contains the CO_2 gas at a high pressure, usually in the region of 600–1000psi at room temperature. Smaller CO_2 kits come supplied with a smaller disposable cylinder, which is discarded after use and replaced with a new cylinder. Larger kits use a refillable CO_2 cylinder that is exchanged for a full cylinder when empty. For larger aquariums, I recommend obtaining the biggest refillable cylinder you can fit inside your cabinet, as this is the most economical

Disposable CO$_2$ cylinders are ideal for smaller planted aquariums.

option. A popular option in the UK is to use CO$_2$ fire extinguishers as a pressurized CO$_2$ cylinder. I usually use a 6 pound (3 kilogram) refillable bottle that requires exchanging every four to five months in my 85-gal (320-L) aquascape. Small nano tanks are more suited to smaller disposable cylinders where space can be limited and are more economically viable.

REGULATOR

The regulator is usually the most expensive and complex component in the CO$_2$ system. It is responsible for reducing the dangerously high pressure of the cylinder contents to a safe working pressure. The working pressure is typically between 20–60 psi, and can be adjusted if you have a dual-stage regulator.

The cheaper single-stage regulators usually have a fixed working pressure that can fluctuate depending

A basic single stage regulator with needle valve that fits to a disposable CO$_2$ cylinder.

on the contents' pressure of the cylinder. For this reason, it is advisable to opt for the dual-stage regulator (if possible). The regulator usually shows two indicator dials: a contents pressure (how much CO$_2$ gas remains in the cylinder) and a working pressure (how much CO$_2$ pressure is available to the aquarium). Many dual stage regulators also have an integrated solenoid, bubble counter, and needle valve fitted—more on these later.

A dual-stage CO_2 regulator with adjustable working pressure, solenoid, needle valve, non-return valve, and bubble counter.

Needle Valve

Attached to the regulator is a needle valve, which allows for fine adjustment of the CO_2 output. Small CO_2 gas flow adjustments can be made by carefully rotating the

Needle valves are used to provide fine adjustment of CO_2 flow.

valve, and the amount is usually witnessed via a bubble counter. Some needle valves are more sensitive than others. Usually, more expensive needle valves allow for finer adjustment, with cheaper models giving big changes in flow with only minimal movements.

Bubble Counter

Bubble counters provide a visual indication of the rate of CO_2 that is flowing through the regulator to the diffuser.

This device is a small vessel usually made from a clear plastic (or sometimes glass) that's partially filled with water or another non-toxic clear liquid substance. The CO_2 gas flows into it and creates bubbles, the rate of which determine the quantity of CO_2 you are adding. Bubble counters can vary in size and style, with a range of different size bubbles being produced. This is important to note when comparing your bubble rate with someone else's CO_2 system that may have a different bubble counter. As a very rough guide, I advise to start off with 1 bubble per second per 20 gal (80 L) of aquarium water and make adjustments as necessary using a CO_2 drop checker or other CO_2 measuring techniques (which will be covered later in this chapter).

Solenoid

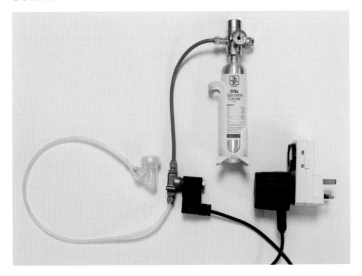

A full CO_2 injection system suitable for small planted aquariums that includes a solenoid and timer to turn the CO_2 on and off automatically.

A solenoid is an electrically operated valve that shuts off CO_2, or lets CO_2 through depending on whether power is applied. When power is applied, the valve is open and CO_2 can flow through. Without power, the CO_2 is stopped.

Solenoids can be integrated as part of the regulator or fitted separately inline between the regulator and bubble counter. Solenoids are useful because we can time the CO_2 to come on and off as necessary. Plants only benefit from CO_2 during lighting, so we can time the solenoid to switch on and off with the lights. A prudent technique is to actually have the solenoid come on *before* the lights. This allows the CO_2 levels to build up prior to the lighting period so the plants can fully utilize the CO_2 straight away. I typically have my CO_2 come on between one to three hours before the lights. The larger the aquarium, the sooner I have the CO_2 activated to allow for sufficient build up.

Non-Return Valve

This is a simple device that is usually located between the diffuser and the regulator to prevent any water from entering into the sensitive mechanical parts of the regulator. Some bubble counters come with a non-return valve fitted.

CO2 Hose

The CO_2 hose is responsible for safely carrying the CO_2 gas through the system. It is usually made from a special material due to the acidic nature of CO_2. Do *not* use cheaper regular tubing that's used for air pumps, as this will degrade over time.

DIFFUSER

The diffuser is the final part of the CO_2 system, and is responsible for the physical delivery of the CO_2 gas into the aquarium water. There are two main types commonly found in aquascaping: the in-tank diffuser and the external inline diffuser.

In-Tank Diffuser

These can be made from a variety of materials, including clear acrylic, glass, and stainless steel. They include a porous ceramic plate that's usually circular in shape where the CO_2 emits from in the form of tiny CO_2

In-tank CO_2 diffusers are best suited to smaller aquascapes. The smaller the CO_2 microbubbles, the more efficient their diffusion and distribution.

microbubbles. The microbubbles float into the aquarium and will ideally get circulated around the entire tank. If you read the section on circulation, you will know why this is important, so that all of the plants can equally benefit from the CO_2. There are different qualities of CO_2 diffuser plants, with the best providing the smallest microbubbles. The smaller the microbubbles, the more efficient the diffusion and distribution of the CO_2 will be. Larger bubbles tend to shoot straight to the aquarium surface before they have a chance to dissolve or reach any plants. Keeping your diffuser clean is important to ensure the microbubbles remain small. (We will cover how to maintain your diffuser in the Maintenance chapter.)

In-tank diffusers are more suited to smaller aquariums, up to 30 gal (120 L). Having one much bigger for this sized aquarium can make it challenging to achieve sufficient distribution of the CO_2 microbubbles. Different sizes of diffusers are available to suit a variety of tank sizes and, interestingly, some of the less expensive types can be more efficient than their more expensive countertypes. Most in-tank diffusers require less CO_2 gas pressure when compared with external in-line diffusers and can be used with cheaper single stage regulators and even yeast-based systems (also covered later).

External In-Line Diffusers and Reactors

An external in-line diffuser is designed to be fitted on the outlet hose of an external canister filter. To apply correctly, you will need to make a cut in the filter hose and fit the diffuser in-between the two newly exposed through a porous ceramic material. The CO_2 microbubbles then get picked up by the flowing water from the filter and into the aquarium via the outlet hose end. This CO_2 "mist" then gets circulated around the aquarium and, if you have a sufficiently powerful filter and have positioned the outlet appropriately, you will see a fine mist of CO_2 microbubbles floating around the entire aquarium.

This mist is virtually invisible in most circumstances. The higher quality the ceramics in your diffuser, the smaller the microbubbles and more efficient the CO_2 distribution and diffusion will be. Most external diffusers require a higher working pressure than in-tank diffusers, and you may need a dual stage regulator to adjust to a higher pressure; typically a minimum of 30 psi is required. The main disadvantage of the external diffuser is that it slightly restricts flow from the filter, so you may need to opt

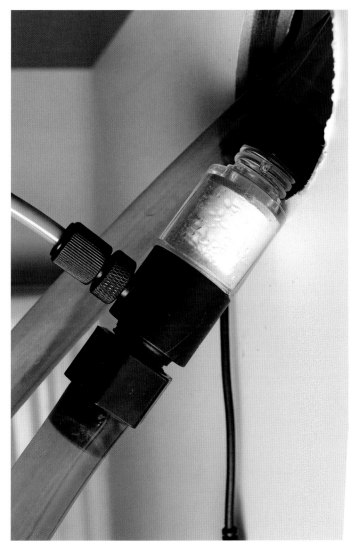

An external in-line CO_2 diffuser attached to the outlet hose of an external filter provides a very fine CO_2 mist that is easily circulated throughout the aquarium.

ends. The external diffuser works on a similar principle to the in-tank diffuser, where the CO_2 gas penetrates

The very fine CO_2 mist flows out from this glass lily pipe filter outlet. The more powerful your external filter flow rate the better your CO_2 will be circulated.

for a more powerful filter to achieve effective overall circulation. The diffuser should also be cleaned regularly to maintain maximum flow efficiency. I make sure to clean mine every time I clean my clear filter hoses.

External Reactors

These work slightly differently to the external diffusers in that they rely on 100 percent dissolution of the CO_2 gas into the water before being delivered to the aquarium. It's usually a much bigger device which often contains plastic balls or ceramic rings with a large surface area (often ceramic biological filter is used). They are fitted in the same way as the external diffuser to the filter hose, and the CO_2 gets pumped into the reactor. The contact time between the CO_2 and water is increased due to the amount of media inside the reactor, allowing for 100 percent CO_2 dissolution. This CO_2 enriched water then flows into the aquarium with no visible bubbles. External reactors are usually more popular with much larger aquariums where circulating a CO_2 microbubble mist may be challenging. They are also useful for folks who prefer not to see any visible bubbles floating around their aquascape.

YEAST-BASED CO2 SYSTEMS

For those on a smaller budget and with smaller aquariums, the yeast-based CO_2 system is a more affordable option to inject CO_2. They work on the principle of combining yeast, sugar, and water (and sometimes bicarbonate of soda) in a sealed container. Fermentation

then occurs, and the result is a production of CO_2 gas. This is then delivered to the aquarium via hose and an in-tank diffuser. The CO_2 pressure is relatively low from yeast-based production, so an appropriate in-tank diffuser is required in order for the CO_2 to pass through. Very basic diffuser types include an upturned bell-shape vessel that sits inside the aquarium and fills with the CO_2 gas. This CO_2 gas pocket inside the bell gradually dissolves into the aquarium water. The main disadvantages of yeast-based systems are their low CO_2 output and uncontrollable nature. Changes in ambient temperature may produce fluctuations in CO_2 output, and the overall lifespan of the yeast-based solution varies accordingly, with output dropping off toward the end of its life. When I started my journey into aquascaping, I used two separate yeast-based systems and switched the mixtures alternately to help ensure a more consistent output. I used a ladder-style diffuser that works by having the CO_2 bubbles enter the bottom of a ladder and rising up in an inverted cascade manner.

PRO TIP: DIY CO2

The lifespan of a yeast-based system depends on the quantities and ratios of the ingredients, as well as the ambient temperature. Using a standard recipe of ½ tsp of yeast, 1 tsp of bicarbonate of soda, and 17 oz (500 ml) of water at 68°F/20°C, you can expect CO_2 production to last around a week. This duration can vary considerably depending on the quality of the yeast and the pH and hardness of the water used in the mixture.

The bubbles gradually dissolve as they rise up through the diffuser.

CO2 TESTING

Measuring CO_2 in your aquarium can be a challenge in order to get an accurate reading due to the unstable nature of the dissolved gas in the water. However, it is important to obtain an approximate measurement, as excess CO_2 is toxic to livestock and can cause a lack of appetite, lethargy, and ultimately death if overdosed. Too little CO_2 and your plants will not benefit fully, with algae a potential consequence.

THE PH DIFFERENTIAL METHOD

This is a simple and effective method to test for CO_2. You need a low-range pH test kit that typically tests between pH 6.0 and 7.6. The pH is a measurement of how acidic or alkaline the water is and is one of the more common tests done by aquarists. CO_2 gas is converted to carbonic acid in the aquarium water, and it's this relationship that can help us measure the presence of CO_2. The more CO_2 there is, the more acidic the water becomes; therefore, the lower the pH.

To start, test the aquarium water pH just before CO_2 is added. If you are running your CO_2 24/7, then you will need to turn it off for at least 12 hours beforehand. A trick is to use a lot of aquarium water surface agitation to help drive off the CO_2 more quickly.

Test the pH of the water after the CO_2 has been added for at least four hours.

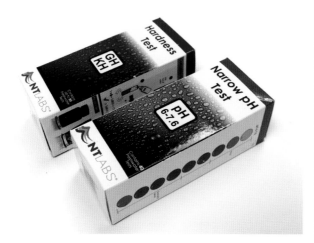

Cross referencing pH and KH test results was the original way to test for CO_2.

Red too much CO_2	
Green ideal CO_2	
Blue too little CO_2	
pH difference	CO_2 present (ppm)
1.5	95
1.4	75
1.3	60
1.2	47
1.1	38
1	30
0.9	24
0.8	19
0.7	15
0.6	12
0.5	9.5
0.4	7.5
0.3	6
0.2	5
0.1	4

Calculate the difference between the two readings and cross-reference to the table below for an approximate CO_2 reading.

For example, if you test your aquarium water pH with the CO_2 on and your test kit reads pH 6.6, then test with the CO_2 off and you get pH 7.6, the difference is 1. Looking at the table, this equates to a CO_2 level of 30 ppm, which is ideal. Higher than this is potentially dangerous to the livestock, and much lower than this can be detrimental to the plants, as shown below.

CO₂ DROP CHECKER METHOD

This is a very simple way to visually see how much CO_2 is present, but note that it is not as accurate as the pH differential method. It relies on a small vessel known

Too little Co₂. Increase Co₂ bubble rate gradually and monitor any color change.

Ideal Co₂ level. Make a note of the Co₂ bubble rate and keep constant.

Too much Co₂. Reduce bubble rate and observe for any ill-effect on fish and shrimp. Perform large water change if required.

as a drop checker which is usually glass and sits inside the aquarium. The drop checker is filled with a special solution (pH reagent and reference 4dKH water solution) that's supplied with most drop checker kits. The solution then changes color depending on how much CO_2 is present in the water. A yellow color indicates too much CO_2 (over 30 ppm), green is good CO_2 (20–30 ppm), and blue is too little CO_2 (under 20 ppm). The disadvantage of this method is that the color can take a long time to change, and the colors themselves are not binary, i.e., there's an infinite amount of shades and hues between each color. However, they are a great way to constantly monitor approximately how much CO_2 you have present. It is also important to note that they can take several hours to indicate any change of CO_2 in the aquarium.

PRO TIP: TESTING VS. MONITORING YOUR CO_2 LEVELS

The drop checker method is a great way to monitor CO_2 levels at a glance. They will indicate instantly to you if you have drastically too much or too little CO_2 present. For more accurate results, the pH testing method is desirable. I like to use the pH method when setting up my CO_2 kit for the first time in order to set the correct bubble rate for my CO_2 injection system. Once this has been set, then there is usually little need to adjust it so you can then use the drop checker to provide peace of mind.

CO2 AND STABILITY

One of the key factors for ensuring success with your aquarium plants and helping to prevent algae growth is the importance of a stable and consistent CO_2 level. Large fluctuating levels of CO_2 are a known algae trigger, with plants adapting to a specific level of CO_2. If the CO_2 supplied is very different from this adapted level, the plant can struggle, leaving the door open to algae. There are devices used to monitor and control the CO_2 automatically, which rely on a pH probe connected to a controller and solenoid. The CO_2 is activated and deactivated in accordance with the pH level. These are usually expensive and can bring up more issues than they solve, with the regular calibration of the pH probes being necessary and the constant on/ off cycle resulting in potentially unstable levels of CO_2. My personal advice is to use a pressurized system with a solenoid on a timer, as discussed.

FINAL WORD ON CO2

If you do take the step into CO_2 injection, you can expect a huge improvement in plant growth and health. It's not for everyone, but if you wish to explore a much wider range of opportunities with plant species and the joy these can provide, then it is worth consideration.

CHAPTER SIX
HOW TO AQUASCAPE

In the previous chapters we explained how to grow plants from a technical point of view by covering low and high-energy systems, lighting, filtration and circulation, nutrients and CO_2. Now comes creative part of how we can use these components and our knowledge of them to help grow our plants and create beautiful aquascapes! Aquascaping should be a joyous process, allowing you to be as creative as you wish. It is important to note that the advice in the pages that follow are only guidelines, and you may wish to tread your own and distinct creative path. Indeed, I would encourage you be as bold as you dare! However, for beginners it can be helpful to follow a few basic rules to help you create something that is likely going to be visually appealing and well balanced. Once you have mastered the basics of creating an attractive design *and* the ability to grow your plants in an aquascape free from algae issues, you are then open to the boundless creative expression of becoming an aquascaper.

PRACTICE

"More aquascaping makes you a better aquascaper."

If I could only give one piece of advice about aquascaping, it would be that the single-best way improve is by practicing. Making mistakes is an essential component for you to grow as an aquascaper, and the more mistakes you make the more you will learn. Do not be afraid of trying anything, so long as you take appropriate responsibility for the welfare of your aquascape's inhabitants. I always recommend that beginners should use books (like this one), magazines, and the web for inspiration. Googling "aquascape" will throw up literally millions of results—12.5 million to be exact at the time of this writing! There is nothing wrong with directly copying someone else's aquascape if you are stuck for your own ideas. You are going to have much more likelihood of creating something you like the look of, and if you can find out the techniques, plants species and equipment used you will have an even greater chance of achieving a beautiful aquascape that you love. We live in an age of social media and it is very possible to go online, join a group or forum, engage with the community, and even seek some form of mentorship. Check out the final chapter for my recommended forums and Facebook groups you may want to consider.

PATIENCE

"The tougher the journey the sweeter the destination."

My second biggest piece of advice would be to learn patience with aquascaping. Delaying gratification is a huge part of long-term success, and it's wise to not expect stunning results right away. Creating the hardscape layout (more on this soon) can provide instant impact, but it's only when the plants have matured, you've maintained them over the weeks and months, done the water changes, dosed the fertilizer, trimmed the growth, cleaned off the algae, and changed the water so many times that you can truly appreciate the well-earned beauty of this slice of nature that you have created. If you struggle with a plant or suffer with algae issues, try not to give up. Do some research (like reading this book) and you should be able to figure out where you need to make adjustments in your aquarium and approach. Correcting some issues can take weeks, so stick with it. Then, when the issue is finally resolved, you will have a much greater sense of satisfaction. I have lost count of the amount of times I have come close to tearing down a complete aquascape due to algae issues. But I resist the urge, do the water changes, pay more attention to adding fertilizers, clean the filter more often and, sure enough, a couple of weeks later, the aquascape is algae free and looking better than ever. I never regret being persistent in the pursuit of success but have sure regretted impulsive strip downs of potentially great aquascapes!

STARTING OUT

"Outline your expectations—make them realistic and achievable."

Simple aquascape designs with easy plants are a great entry-route for beginners.

Creating your first aquascape is an exciting time, but it can be a bit daunting. There's literally infinite creative potential, so it's important to have a clear idea of your end goal. This is why looking at other aquascapes for inspiration is a good idea for many, especially if you are like me without a strong imagination or visualization skills. Some aquascapers like to use landscapes, seascapes, mountain ranges or scenes from forests as inspiration. This is great advice, and no matter where you gain your inspiration from, the most important part of the journey is to have fun and enjoy it.

I do recommend starting off relatively simple. If

you were a brand new piano player and just bought your first keyboard, it would be unrealistic to be able to play the standard of a professional pianist right away. It takes lots of practice and, you guessed it, patience. Consider beginning with simple hardscape layouts and growing easy plants. Master the plant growing, gardening, and maintenance stage, and when you're capable of growing your plants without algae you can progress to more complex aquascape designs. It shouldn't take long if you've invested in the appropriate equipment and followed the advice from the earlier chapters in this book. As you gain more confidence growing a wider range of aquarium plants and experimenting with different layout materials and styles, you will naturally evolve and begin to tread your own path. You may still use design elements from those early aquascapes that you may have copied—I still very much use the classic Nature Aquarium style, pioneered by the late Takashi Amano, almost twenty years after beginning my hobby. There is no defined path to creating a successful aquascape but you will know when *you* have had success because you can see and feel it for yourself. I am so excited for you to feel this sense of accomplishment when you create your first successful aquascape, because I remember exactly how great it felt!

COMPOSITION

Composition is the art of arranging all of the aquarium's interior components such as wood, rocks, and plants, as well as the use of open space, light, and shade. We could place our wood, rocks, and plants randomly and hope for the best. You may get very lucky and create something beautiful, but it will be unlikely. You may also possess a natural artistic flair and sensitivity that results in you effortlessly positioning these components without any real conscious thought and come up with a masterpiece. For most of us, though, it is prudent to consider some compositional guidelines that will help greatly in ensuring your aquascaping gives a pleasant impression and visual balance.

RULE OF THIRDS

My favorite compositional guideline—and the most basic—is the rule of thirds. Those of you with smart phones may have already witnessed this in action with the overlaid grid formation on the screen when using the phone's camera. The screen, or in our case the aquarium, is divided into three equal sections, both horizontally and vertically. The result is four

Most smartphone camera apps come with a rule of thirds overlay making them easy to compose your image.

intersections around the center of the aquarium. If we now position our main focal point of the aquascape, i.e., the most dominant aspect such as a large stone, piece of wood, or bright red plant on any of those four intersections, then we should achieve a pleasant, visual balance. Using the rule of thirds can be very helpful when first installing the hardscape and planting with attention being paid to positioning these components. Red plants are an eye-catcher and therefore a focal point, so it can be a good idea to plant these approximately one third from the left- or right-hand sides of the aquarium edge. The same principle applies to position of the most impactful rocks or wood.

GOLDEN RATIO AND CIRCLES

Golden ratio lines and circles are useful for positioning focal points in the hardscape.

The golden ratio is quite similar to the rule of thirds in that the aquarium can be split visually into different sections and we can use these to position our focal points. The mathematics are more complex and were originally identified by Leonardo Fibonacci. Interestingly the golden ratio can be found in many cases in nature, i.e., the spiral in snail shells, flower petals, seed heads, and even hurricanes (viewed from above). The actual ratio is expressed as 1:1.618 (to three decimal places).

GUIDELINES ONLY

While these guidelines can be useful for positioning our focal points, it is important to note that if your aquascape does not strictly conform to the rule of thirds or golden ratio then it does not necessarily mean it will look ugly. Remember that it is your own aquascape, and if you like how it looks, and your plants/fish are happy and healthy, then that is the most important aspect. Also consider that, as the plants grow and mature, the entire composition of the aquascape can shift and you do have an element of control over this by appropriate trimming and potential repositioning of plants and hardscape if so desired. Aquascaping is a constantly evolving and organic art form, and it's this gradual progression that is one of the most fascinating parts to the hobby. I often witness budding aquascapers showing off their newly planted aquascapes with perhaps less than perfect hardscape composition, but I know in several weeks that whole composition will change significantly due to how the plants influence the overall visual balance. With purposeful trimming

techniques, the aquascape can change quite dramatically from something that looks okay to something quite beautiful.

USE OF DEPTH IS A GAME CHANGER

The highest impact aquascapes often succeed by creating a great sense of depth.

One of the biggest lessons in aquascaping that I have learned in recent years how the effective use of depth can really bring an aquascape to life. I have studied literally thousands of aquascapes through books, magazines, and the web, and have been grateful to be a judge on several international aquascaping contests; both live and via photographs. I can conclude that the most impressive aquascapes are those that have really focused and executed well on the use of creating depth. I refer to depth in terms of how deep the aquascape appears from front to back, not height. This is particularly impressive and important when viewing the aquascape in two dimensions via print or electronic media. When viewing many professional level aquascapes, you may notice several distinct sections to the aquascape ranging from foreground to background. In contrast, many beginner aquascapes tend to look relatively flat when viewed directly from the front. There are a few techniques that we can employ to help enhance this sense of depth.

TIPS FOR CREATING DEPTH IN YOUR AQUASCAPE

1. Slope the substrate toward the rear. This creates and optical illusion when viewing the aquascape directly from the front that it's much deeper (front to back) than it really is. The steeper the slope, the more pronounced this illusion. Be mindful that excess depth without planting can potentially cause an excess in anaerobic bacteria and toxic hydrogen sulfide. This risk is reduced significantly if a complete soil is used in conjunction with oxygen production from the plant roots. Species such as *Cryptocoryne* have particularly great root system and you could also consider stocking Malaysian trumpet snail (*Melanoides tuberculatus*) to help keep the substrate aerated (although there is always a risk of over-population with these snails).

2. Divide the aquascape from front to rear by using foreground, midground, and background elements. Each of these can be split further. For example, you could have five species of plants and different hardscape elements spanning from the front to the rear of the aquarium. Consider how these combine to give the overall desired effect.

3. A popular technique in modern aquascaping is to deliberately use broader-leaved plants in the foreground, such as *Micranthemum* "Monte Carlo," followed by smaller-leaved plants in the background, such as *Hemianthus callitrichoides* "Cuba." If the overall shape of the leaves are similar, this can create an illusion of enhanced depth. Consider three or more species with similar shaped leaves running through the aquascape for maximum effect.

4. Pathways leading through an aquascape are a very effective way to lead the viewer's eye. They are often created by using a cosmetic inert sand or fine gravel that runs from the front of the aquarium all the way to the rear. This gives the unmistakable impression of how deep the aquascape is, and if this effect is further enhanced with the use of a deep substrate in the rear, the overall effect can be very dramatic. A common technique to sloping the substrate is to use an inert bulking material underneath the soil, such as lava stones or net bags full of ceramic filter media. This also has the advantage of saving cost, as these items are cheaper than the soil.

5. The deliberate use of shadows is a great way to provide contrast in an aquascape. Overhanging rocks or large plants that block light from above create dark areas in the aquascape, and it's this contrast between the brightly lit and colorful plants around it that can add great contrast and impact.

Shadows created by overhanging plants here create dramatic contrast in light and shade.

COLORS AND TEXTURES

Colors and textures provide visual interest to an aquascape. Consider the colors of the hardscape and how it contrasts with the plants, then consider how the plants colors and textures contrast with each other. This is particularly important when looking at plants that are next to each other. For example, having two red plant species next to each other would be less impactful than having the two species separated by other plants. It may be your intention to deliberately create a more subtle blend of colors and textures that flow into each other, or you may want to create a real sense of drama by deliberately using contrasting species adjacent to one another. Think about the overall story you are trying to tell with your aquascape and the impression you want to achieve to anyone viewing the tank. A good example is to contrast two very distinct styles. Imagine an Iwagumi with just the one species of carpeting plant and three stones next to a Dutch style aquascape. They are both beautiful in their own way, but hugely different in the stories and feelings they are conveying.

AQUASCAPING STYLES

Aquascaping can be broadly split into several styles, and please note that these style definitions are based on my own interpretation of this art. As with all art forms, aquascaping is subjective and in some respects there is no style that's better than another—it's a matter of taste and sensitivity. The styles can also be described as non-linear, with many crossing over one another in some respects. For example, a biotope aquascape—one that aims to replicate a natural habitat—may use elements of the Nature Aquarium style due to the inclusion of natural materials in a specific composition.

Dutch Style

The Dutch style of aquascaping started in the 1930s and follows a strict set of rules that were originally

A stunning example of a Dutch aquascape created by US aquascaper Joe Harvey.

outlined by the Dutch Society for Aquarists (NBAT) in 1956. The overall principle of Dutch aquascaping is the focus on formal groups of plants, with attention being paid to their colors and textures and how they are positioned in and around the aquarium. The style is similar to formal landscape gardens and flowerbeds that are commonplace in some parts of the world. I really admire the technical skill and attention to detail that goes into creating and maintaining these visually stunning aquariums. Some aquascapers, however, find them a little too formal without much room for more loosely expressing nature.

Tips for Dutch Aquascaping

1. Before you attempt a Dutch aquascape, it may be a good idea to really hone your plant growing and trimming skills—especially with stem plants.
2. Do your research and analyze the best Dutch aquascapes out there for inspiration.
3. Practice, and be patient!

The Aquatic Gardener's Association International Aquascaping (AGA) Contest includes a Dutch aquascape category with some great examples (see link to the AGA at the end of this book).

There is a great online article on the UK Aquatic Plant Society (UKAPS) forum (see link to UKAPS at the end of this book).

A 7500-gallon Asian river-themed aquascape featuring all plants and fish from Southeast Asia.

Biotope Aquascapes

Biotope aquascapes are designed to mimic a fish's natural habitat. Research is carried out on the specific region, with attention being paid to various aspects such as water chemistry and temperature, water flow rate, and depth. Lakes, rivers, or streams from all over the world can be simulated to great effect and interest. Substrate types and other natural materials, as such leaf litter, wood, or rocks are replicated. Some biotopes have aquatic plants, and correct species should be used. The materials are often laid out in the aquarium to enhance the overall impression with attention

This blackwater Amazon River–themed aquascape uses botanicals and driftwood to deliberately stain the water.

being paid to focal points, visual balance, use of texture, and sometimes color. Blackwater biotopes are becoming very popular with the deliberate use of tannin-stained water; a result of decomposing materials such as leaf litter and soft wood. I really enjoy these aquascapes particularly because of the way the fish look and behave. Their colors are usually much more pronounced, and breeding behaviors are encouraged due to their natural conditions. I also appreciate that, through today's rampant deforestation and natural habitat destruction, biotope aquascapes can be an important tool to educate those that are otherwise unaware of these issues.

Tips for Biotope Aquascaping

1. Figure out which fish you'd like to keep and what habitat you want to create.
2. Do your research and find out the water parameters and temperature of the natural waters of that fish.
3. Research any plants that may grow in the habitat and try to source some from a high-quality source.
4. Use the same types of substrate materials if possible, i.e., same color and texture sand or gravel.
5. Try to find similar hardscape materials to what is naturally found in the habitat, i.e., same types of wood, rock, leaf litter, etc.
6. Consider the water movement in the aquarium, i.e., a lake habitat will have less circulation than a fast-flowing stream.
7. Lighting levels and types of lighting are important. Is the habitat shaded or in open space? Shallower waters should have brighter lighting than fish found in deep or canopy-covered waters.

There are some links to biotope aquarium websites at the end of this book.

Jungle Style

The jungle style is probably the loosest style in terms of rules—there really aren't any! Those no strict guidelines, there are common themes often seen in these aquascapes, namely the dense planting and use of broader leaf plants, such as *Apongogeton* and large *Echinodorus* species. Little or no open space is kept with, perhaps, little observation paid toward using

The potted plants on either side of this aquascape add to the jungle style theme. This aquascape was created for the Scaped Nature store in England by the author.

typical foreground to background planting arrangements. Chaos is the order of the day here, and for this reason it is a popular style for beginners who are unsure of what their end goal or vision might be. There is nothing wrong with this and jungle style aquascapes are often a great way for the aquascaper to understand what plants work well and not so well in that specific set-up. Some of my own personal favorite aquascapes have been jungle style just for the fun element of not worrying as much about composition or how the plants are trimmed. Most fish thrive in jungle aquascapes due to the amount of plants offering shade, shelter, and security. Algae issues are usually

The overgrown and almost chaotic nature of this aquascape gives a great jungle vibe.

less commonplace due to the often large nutrient uptake from so many plants, and for this reason liquid fertilizer dosing is more important than aquariums with less plant density. Floating plants are often used to further enhance the jungle theme—especially with species that have longer dangling roots, such as *Limnobium laevigatum*. These are also perfect breeding grounds for many fish species. What I really love about jungle aquascapes is their ability to look good even with neglectful trimming. In fact, this unkempt look almost adds to their charm. Care does need to be taken to ensure the lower plants are not starved of light from the taller plants that will shade them, and the same principle needs to be applied with the floating plants.

Tips for Jungle Aquascaping

1. Plant heavily from the outset with as many healthy plants as you can.
2. Consider foreground, midground, and background species, but don't be afraid to experiment!
3. Use floating plants—especially at the beginning. These can help prevent algae in the early stages due to their shading and fast growth.
4. Let it grow, and don't overly be concerned with trimming back plants too much.
5. Enjoy the chaos!

LOW-TECH STYLE

We have already discussed the difference between low- and high-energy planted aquariums, but it is worth talking about low-energy—also known as low-tech

A fine example of a low-tech aquascape with no CO_2 injection and easy plants.

aquariums—with specific reference to their aquascaping style. It can be said that it is possible to create a low-energy aquascape in any style but there is a common theme with many aquascapers utilizing this approach. The biggest driving factor is the plant choice because it is limited with the lower levels of lighting, non-CO_2 injection and lower nutrient levels. Epiphyte species that attach to the decor (hardscape) are ideal as most of these are tolerant of lower lighting. Classic species include *Anubias* and *Microsorum* with background plants consisting of easy stem plants such as *Hygrophila* or *Vallisneria*. (A comprehensive list of plants can be found in a later chapter.) Foreground plants are less often used due to their further distance from the light but some easy species such as *Cryptocoryne parva* or *Marsilea* make ideal candidates. *Echinodorus* also make ideal candidates for larger low-tech tanks.

Tips for Low-Tech Aquascaping
1. Choose *only* easy plant species.
2. If possible, invest in a nutrient-rich substrate. They can be more expensive, but the results are far superior to using plain inert gravel or sand. Root capsules or tablets are an ideal substrate supplement.
3. Don't overstock with fish. The nutrient uptake of the plants is much slower in a low-tech planted aquarium, so fish waste will accumulate more quickly.
4. Avoid excess light. Without CO_2 injection, too much light will rapidly induce an algae bloom, as the plants are not capable of growing enough to keep up with demand. Struggling plants result in more algae!
5. Be patient. Plant growth is typically up to 10x slower in a non-CO_2 injected aquarium.

NATURE STYLE

This is my favorite style, and at the time of writing the Nature Aquarium is the most popular aquascaping style in the world. The creator of the Nature Aquarium concept was Japanese aquarist Takashi Amano, who sadly passed on August 4, 2015, at the age of sixty-one.

The world's largest Nature Aquarium, holding 40,000 gallons, was created by the godfather of modern aquascaping, Takashi Amano.

Amano revolutionized the way we think about aquariums, which most of us now take for granted. He was the first aquarist to skillfully blend the use of natural materials—wood, rocks, and live plants—in a manner that replicated slices of nature, from rocky landscapes to forests. Combined with his skills as an award-winning professional photographer and setting up his own aquascaping brand, Aqua Design Amano (ADA), Amano took the world by storm with his groundbreaking aquascapes and published several aquascaping books and a monthly magazine, *Aqua Journal*.

A classic style Nature Aquarium aquascape photographed in the author's local aquascaping store, Aquarium Gardens.

ADA still thrives today and are highly regarded as the world's premium aquascape brand, hosting the world's largest aquascaping contest, the International Aquatic Plant Layout Contest (IAPLC). This contest is entered by thousands every year from over sixty countries with a top prize of 1,000,000 Yen (approximately US $10,000 at the time of writing). Entrants send in photographs of their aquascapes and they are judged by an esteemed panel of international aquarium industry professionals. You can find a link to some of the previous winners at the end of this book.

For many serious aquascapers, ranking highly in this contest is regarded as the ultimate goal with incredible efforts going into creating and photographing the best aquascapes possible. Each year, new innovations are seen that can potentially set new trends in the aquascaping hobby. It's almost like a car show when you see the crazy-looking concept cars, with some of the design aspects and technologies trickling down to the mainstream. If you are a beginner, I think it's great to be inspired by these aquascapes. However, it can also be a little overwhelming if that's the level that you believe you should be at. I refer back to my earlier point of starting off with simple designs and easy plants and gradually evolving your own style as you gain more experience and confidence. There's no race, so enjoy the process at your own speed.

The Nature Aquarium style can be broken down into three different sub-styles.

Ryoboku Style (Wood-Based)

This aquascape style is based on using wood as the main hardscape material. Stones can also be used, but these are not the main focus. There are many types of wood that can be used, which will be discussed later such as driftwood, bogwood, Manzanita wood and Redmoor roots. Often the wood will protrude from the water surface which adds an enhanced sense of nature. Mosses and other epiphyte plants are also commonly used, adding a beautiful sense of maturity and aged appearance. Only one type of wood is usually used, as this looks more natural. However, it is becoming more commonplace to add very fine details with tiny branches, often in a dropping vertical style mimicking dangling vines or creeping roots attached to the broader wood pieces. It is worth considering exactly how much wood you want to use in the aquascape and to think about how it will look once the plants have grown—especially when

Driftwood dominates this Ryoboku Style aquascape that was created during a workshop by the author for the world-famous Green Aqua store in Hungary.

using epiphytes. Often, a mature aquascape will have its wood completely hidden by the planting. Choosing a wood type can be confusing for beginners, but my tip would be to ensure the chosen wood has a strong visual impact and fills a good amount of space in the aquarium. Try to avoid pieces of wood with clean off-cuts, as these can look unnatural and spoil the overall aesthetic.

Tips for a Ryoboku Aquascape

Carefully select your wood in terms of size, shape, and type. Ensure it's tall and bold enough.

1. Do not mix types of wood unless you are adding small detail pieces that complement the larger pieces.
2. Consider focal points. The most impactful part of the wood will draw the eye, so position it carefully.
3. Some wood will float upon first installation, so pre-soaking it or weighing it down may be necessary.
4. Many types of wood will leech tannins and stain the water. If this isn't desired, then pre-soaking or adding chemical filtration in combination with plenty of large water changes will help.
5. You may occasionally experience harmless white fungal growth on some wood types after initial installation. This can be removed with a toothbrush and rarely returns.
6. Keep the wood clean if possible to avoid algae

build up. Algae-eating shrimp and snails are a great option.

7. If you are growing moss on the wood then keep it well-trimmed to promote compact and healthy growth.

Iwagumi Style (Rock-Based)

Iwagumi roughly translates from the Japanese term "rock garden," and is one of the most well-known and popular styles of Nature Aquarium aquascapes due to its relative simplicity and zen-like appearance. Rocks are the only hardscape material used, and selection of the rock types and sizes must be carefully considered in order to achieve the best results. It can be a rather deceptive style for beginners because of the simple nature of the layout. However, when only using one material and usually a limited, sometimes single plant species, there is no room to hide; a slightly misplaced stone will stand out like a sore thumb. This lesson

Iain Sutherland's stunning Iwagumi aquascape.

can be applied to any aquascape in that the simpler the composition and fewer range of plants, the more challenging it can be to create a really well-balanced aquascape—consider this when planning your aquascape, no matter the style you are going for. A common theme for Iwagumi aquascapes is usually just the one type of stone or rock which is used. Plant species are often limited, too, with minimalist styles employing just one carpeting species (such as *Hemianthus callitrichoides* "Cuba"). An important aspect of any Nature Aquarium style aquascape is using lessons from nature in order to create the most natural-looking aquascape. For instance, it is rare to find two distinctly different types of stones in the same location in nature. When selecting your stones, it is a great idea to start off with a main focal point stone, which is usually much bigger than the others. Then choose progressively smaller stones, usually ending in odd numbers, such as 3, 5, 7, etc. The main stone is often placed in accordance with the rule of thirds—or golden section—with the smaller supporting stones positioned to achieve an ideal balance. A lot of stones will have a distinct strata. These are the natural lines that have been cast into the stone, and we can use these lines to our advantage by having them point in a certain direction. They can oppose each other, often at right angles, which creates a sense of tension, or they can be deliberately placed in the same direction to create a sense of flow. Plant choice in Iwagumi aquascapes is usually based on low-growing carpeting plants, which create a lawn effect. These can be slow growing to start with and may provide a larger

Dominating Frodo Stones are used in this Iwagumi aquascape to create high impact.

This moss-only aquascape uses fine textures to create a great sense of scale.

risk of algae. This can be mitigated by employing large, frequent water changes in combination with a large population of algae-eating shrimp and snails, such as Amano shrimp (*Caridina multidentate*) and Nerite snails (*Neritina Natalensis*).

Appropriate CO_2 management and circulation levels are paramount in an Iwagumi because the plants are typically so low down in the water column.

Tips for an Iwagumi Aquascape

1. Use only one type of stone for the entire aquarium.
2. Slope the substrate so it is deeper at the rear of the aquarium to create an added sense of depth.
3. Ensure the main stone is large enough to create sufficient height and visual impact in the aquarium.
4. Choose the stones carefully to ensure they have interesting character. Spend plenty of time in the store selecting the best stone you can find.
5. Use odd numbers of stones to help avoid symmetry.
6. Pay special attention to positioning the main (biggest) stone, as this is the focal point. The rule of thirds is a good place to start.
7. Use any strata (natural lines) to your advantage by aligning the stone's strata to create a sense of flow, or at right angles to one another in order to create tension.
8. Spend as much time as you need on the stone arrangement while the aquarium is dry with

just the substrate installed. I have taken weeks on one design before, so don't feel as though you need to settle. Remember practice and patience are the cornerstones to successful aquascaping.

9. Be aware that some stones can influence the water chemistry, i.e., boost pH and hardness. Large frequent water changes are often employed to negate this effect.

10. Plant heavily from the outset, typically with carpeting species.

11. Focus on good CO_2 and circulation levels in combination with large, frequent water changes in order to minimize algae.

12. Regularly siphon out excess organic waste accumulation from an established carpet to reduce the risk of algae.

A single species shoal of Black neon tetras add movement and subtle coloration.

Diorama Style

A very popular trend in aquascaping at the time of writing is the diorama style, which uses a physical landscape or fantasy scene as the main source of

This underwater tree with accompanying tiny fish give the illusion of a landscape with birds.

inspiration. Another name often used to describe this style is "georama." These aquascapes typically focus on the hardscape in order to create a landscape effect with planting often limited to very small textures and a few species in order to maintain a sense of scale. The hardscape layouts are often highly complex underwater structures that take months to create with rocks or wood being painstakingly glued together. While I appreciate the level of skill involved with creating and maintaining these aquascapes, my personal taste finds these a little too contrived. For example, when I see the fish swimming in an underwater cave system or forest with bonsai trees, it looks rather odd. However, this style is very high impact and does really grab the attention of the viewer, especially to anyone that's never seen a diorama-style aquascape before. If they can help inspire a generation of new aquascapers, then I am big fan. I have yet to create a diorama style aquascape, as I prefer the more traditional Nature Aquarium style. I find this to be more achievable for new aquascapers relying on more simple hardscape layouts and focusing more on the planting to create both a beautiful and long-term healthy aquascape.

A beautiful hardscape design by Juan Puchades, created for the Spanish PezVerde aquascape store.

CHAPTER SEVEN
HARDSCAPE

Hardscape is the common name given to the decorative materials in the aquarium. In aquascaping, the most commonly used materials are wood and rocks. I like to refer to the hardscape as the backbone of the aquascape. If we can create a high-impact and aesthetically balanced hardscape composition, then we are far more likely to succeed with a beautiful aquascape.

Conversely, if we add only a minimal quantity and small-sized pieces of hardscape with little aesthetic impact, then we have to rely more on the plants to create the overall impact, which can be a lot more challenging. Some styles of aquascaping can only use hardscapes with no planting and still manage to create a

This hardscape-only aquascape on the right contrasts well with the planted aquarium in the background.

beautiful aquarium. These hardscape-only aquascapes are particularly useful for aquariums with herbivorous or boisterous fish, such as goldfish and large cichlids, and for aquarium owners that may not wish to invest in the potentially more expensive equipment and time that are required to succeed with aquarium plants.

For my own aquascaping journey, understanding the importance of hardscape was a real game changer. Back then in the early 2000s, obtaining good quality hardscape materials from a local aquarium store was a case of hit and miss. Thankfully, now hardscape choices are far more abundant—even if you have to source it online. Some web shops even show you the exact pieces you will receive, and even have complete sets of rock and wood combinations designed for specific aquarium sizes. This is great news if you live in a remote area far from an aquarium store, where the journey may be wasted in light of a poor hardscape selection. It is also perfect for beginners who may feel overwhelmed with the quantities of hardscape and combinations available to them.

CHOOSING ROCKS

There are dozens of different rocks types available. I suggest buying rocks from an aquarium store rather than collecting your own to ensure that they are aquarium-safe and to avoid conflicting with any potential laws about removing natural materials from their

Choosing the right type, quantity and size of hardscape is essential to create the best impact.

environment. With dozens of different available rock types to choose from, it may be a little confusing deciding which to go for. Here are some tips to help you choose.

1. Stick to one type of rock throughout the aquascape. Mixing types tends to look more unnatural and can confuse the visual layout.

2. Spend some time looking through the available selection and pick out the best pieces. Look for rocks with the most interesting character that will suit the style of aquascape you intend to create. For example, flat rocks with right angles tend to look more boring than rocks with interesting lines, veins, pitted textures, and interesting shapes.

3. Buy big! One of the most common beginner mistakes in aquascaping is not buying large enough hardscape materials. If you are creating a rock-only or rock-dominated aquascape, then buy at least one large rock. This will form the main focal point to the layout and, ideally, should fill around two-thirds of the aquarium's height. This is where the rule of thirds (that we discussed in the previous chapter) can be helpful.

4. Buy more than you think you will need so you have plenty of options.

5. Consider color. The color of the rock is very important, as it will help to create a theme to your aquascape. For example, Dragon Stone has yellow, orange, and brown tones that can suit an autumnal-style effect. Seiryu Stone is grey and often has white veins that suit a more landscape-type effect.

6. Think textures. Some rocks will have deep gouges and rough textures, whereas others may be smooth boulders or pebbles. Choose the texture according to the overall feel you are trying to convey with your aquascape. For example, smooth rocks often suit aquascapes that mimic a fast-flowing stream or river, as the rocks have been eroded by the water. More jagged rocks tend to suit an aquascape based more on a landscape design.

7. If you are on a tight budget, then consider Lava Stone. This is less dense than other rocks and, as most rocks are sold by weight, you will get more volume of rock for your dollar.

An important detail to keep in mind is that some rocks can affect the aquarium water chemistry. Many types of rocks contain limestone, which can increase pH and hardness while some rock types leech more carbonates than others do. This is not usually an issue if you carry out large and frequent water changes. I like to carry out 50 percent water changes once per week, which helps to reset any increases in pH and hardness. Any water chemistry impact is reduced based upon the hardness that your aquarium water is from the beginning. Very soft aquarium water will see a bigger influence from rocks containing limestone.

It is also important to note that the addition of carbon dioxide injection can often reduce the aquarium water pH to below 7, making it more acidic. This can slowly dissolve the rock and boost the hardness of the water. If in doubt, consider using rocks that do not contain limestone, such as Dragon Stone and Lava Stone. A simple way to test this is to use a strong acid substance, such as Hydrochloric acid, directly onto the rock and look for any fizzing. Do so with caution outside and use appropriate personal protective equipment such as rubber gloves and safety glasses.

While some suppliers may use different names, below are some of the more commonly available rock types:

POSITIONING ROCKS

Ideal rock selection and positioning is particularly important in rock-only aquascapes, as discussed in the previous chapter on Iwagumi-style aquascapes. When positioning your rocks, consider using compositional guidelines such as the rule of thirds. Also consider the rocks' relationships to each other in terms of how their shapes and strata (natural lines) line up or oppose one another. It is often a good idea to partially bury a rock into the substrate instead of having it simply rest on top. This helps to create a more natural appearance as if the rock had been exposed from a landmass after the earth has been gradually eroded after many years. Remember, with aquascaping we are often aiming to replicate a slice of nature and using lessons from nature is the perfect way to help achieve this goal.

Practicing the rock layout in a dry aquarium is highly recommended before you fill with water. This avoids lots of mess! Dedicate some time to fully focusing on creating your best layout possible and try to use the experience to relax and enjoy the creative aspect. I will often enter a state of "flow" during this process, which allows me to be the most creative. If you start to get frustrated and unhappy with how the layout is progressing, then simply step away and return a few hours later. Do not rush this process, because getting the hardscape layout right is the most important first step in creating your aquascape.

Frodo Stone

Black Lava Stone

Millenium Stone

Red Lava Stone

Seiryu Stone (also known as Mini Landscape Rock)

Dragon Stone

Fossilized Wood Stone

Additional Types of Rocks (not pictured):

Grey Mountain Rock Gobi Stone

Glimmer Rock Stonewood

Maple Leaf Rock Yangste Rocks

Knife Stone Galapagos Rock

This wood with its tree trunk effect and trailing roots adds a great natural feel.

CHOOSING WOOD

As with rocks, there any many different types of wood available. For the same reasons listed above, I recommend purchasing your wood from an aquarium retailer. Collecting your own wood can be fine, but there is always a risk of the wood containing some toxins. The main considerations for choosing wood should be the type of impact you wish to create in your aquascape. For example, large bold pieces may be more ideal for a simple style layout, while thinner branches suit a more complex design.

A popular technique for more advanced aquascapers is to mix types of wood to create a more complex and naturalistic design. For example, using fine twigs attached to bigger pieces of wood can create a vine-like epiphytic effect that enhances the overall sense of natural detail. My advice is to buy more pieces of wood than you think you will need and go for a wide selection of sizes. Just make sure to stick to the same type of wood to start with to obtain a more natural look. Different types of wood have different textures and colors, and mixing these often don't look the most coherent.

As with selecting rocks, we are trying to create something similar to what you might see in nature. Huge pieces of wood can look great and provide instant impact while also giving you lots of space to attach epiphyte plants, such as *Microsorum pteropus*, *Anubias*, *Bucephalandra*, and mosses. I love epiphyte plants because they add an immediate sense of maturity and, depending on the plant species and size, can also give you an ideal focal point (but more on choosing plants later). Some wood will leech tannins into the aquarium water that can discolor it a yellow/brown hue. This may be desirable in some cases, especially if you want to create a blackwater-style aquascape. The staining is not harmful to fish, and some species will actually appreciate it. However, most aquascapers prefer clear water, which can be done by pre-soaking the wood for a long period. One advantage to this is that the wood will immediately sink in your new aquascape, whereas many new woods will wish to float and then must be secured in your tank. A common technique I use is to partially bury the wood in the substrate and then strategically place rocks on top of it, ensuring as natural a look as possible.

While some suppliers may use different names, below are some of the more commonly available wood types:

Driftwood
Bogwood
Mopani Wood
Manzanita Wood
Redmoor Wood
Spider Wood
Millenium Wood
Dragon Wood
Iron Wood
River Wood
Structure Wood

PREPARING NEW WOOD FOR AQUASCAPING

1. If you have space, then consider a large water container in your garden or spare room and fill with water. Place your wood inside and place a rock on top to keep it from floating.
2. Once the wood is sinking, then it should be ready. Do not let it dry out, otherwise it may float in your aquascape (a mistake I have made several times!).
3. Place your wood in your aquascape and spray regularly with water to prevent the wood from drying out during the aquascape process.
4. Once the aquarium has filled, monitor the water for any tannin stains. If you prefer clear water, then perform large, frequent water changes and/or use a chemical filtration media such as activated carbon or Seachem Purigen.
5. If you have to use dry wood, then attaching a rock to the bottom of the wood with a zip tie and burying it in the substrate is an option.
6. You can also use a non-toxic waterproof glue, such as JBL Haru to attach the wood to the aquarium base or rocks.

PRO TIP: USE NATURAL-LOOKING WOOD

Try to avoid wood with blunt, manmade sawn-off ends, as these look unnatural. If you are limited to these pieces, then use some bonsai tree snips or similar to roughen up the ends so the wood looks far more natural.

POSITIONING WOOD

Wood is one of the easiest and best ways to provide instant impact in an aquascape. Where the wood is positioned can really make the difference between creating an average aquascape or a great one. It can be overwhelming at first, as there are countless options with working in all axes and in three dimensions. By using the compositional guidelines outlined earlier you should be able to make a good start. As with all hardscaping processes, it's best done in a dry aquarium so there's less mess and you can spend however long you need to get it right. Sometimes photographing each layout attempt can prove useful so you can refer back to them and choose your favorite. As with rock positioning, don't rush it, and if you start to feel frustrated then leave it for a while and only return when you have regained the motivation. Use this process as an opportunity to relax and engage the creative part of your brain. The good news is that if you have some great materials to work with then the layout should come easily. This is why it is essential to invest in good hardscape supplies.

TIPS FOR POSITIONING WOOD

1. Consider the rule of thirds when positioning the largest piece of wood. This is usually the focal point, and so needs to be aesthetically balanced.
2. Think about horizontal and vertical lines. Having wood crisscrossing can look great if done in the right way.
3. Consider how the wood flows across the aquarium. Does it look natural, or is there too much tension in the design?
4. Try to avoid having the wood rest against the aquarium glass, as this can make standard maintenance quite challenging.
5. If you have a rimless open-top aquarium, then consider having some wood protruding from the surface. This can really add a further sense of nature to the aquarium. For added effect, attach some moss that will creep over the surface, too.

Using several smaller wood pieces together to create the illusion of one larger piece is a great idea, especially if you can't find a big piece suitable.

PRO TIP: HOARDING!

When I used to review aquarium stores for *Practical Fishkeeping* magazine, one of my favorite bonus tasks was rummaging through all of the store's hardscape supplies and buying at least one piece of wood or stone for my own personal stash. Over the years I collected some wonderful pieces that currently sit in my garage, ready to be used in future aquascapes. I suggest you do the same . . . if you have space! Creating great aquascapes can only be achieved if you have access to great materials. Invest the time and money into collecting the best pieces you can, and you will then have many more options when the time comes to create a new aquascape.

PRO TIP: CREATE YOUR OWN HARDSCAPE DOJO!

The best way to get better at creating hardscape layouts is to practice! Create a shallow container filled with some sand or gravel at the appropriate size and use this to practice your hardscape layouts. Some aquascaping specialist stores may have these available to use in-store so you can "try before you buy," ensuring you will be happy with your selected materials.

CHAPTER EIGHT
CHOOSING, PREPARING, AND MAINTAINING YOUR AQUARIUM PLANTS

In Chapter One, we briefly discussed the benefits of keeping plants, but how do we know which plants to buy, where to position them in the aquascape, how to prepare them, and how to maintain them? In this chapter we will cover all of these topics so you will know how to get the best out of your plants, consequently enabling you to create a stunning aquascape full of lush and healthy plant growth. There are few things more rewarding than seeing your plants growing to a point where they need trimming, re-planting, and even given away or sold to other hobbyists. If you have already followed the advice in this book, I can almost guarantee you will have success with your plants . . . but before you rush out to your local aquarium store and buy the first plants you see, I encourage you to read the information in this chapter carefully!

BUYING HEALTHY PLANTS

It is essential for me to emphasize the importance in ensuring that the plants you are purchasing are as healthy as possible. A plant that has been neglected prior to you receiving it may struggle to adapt to its new home in your aquarium. A struggling plant will have less chance of being able to fight off algae, which

If you are very lucky (like me!), your local aquarium store will keep their plants in ideal conditions, like these mini greenhouses using hydroponics.

is especially likely in a newly set up aquascape. For this reason, make sure the plants you purchase are as fresh as they can be from your supplier. Unfortunately, many stores do not keep their aquarium plants in ideal conditions, which means that there is a very real likelihood that they may be slowly dying in their holding facility. For this reason, I like to politely speak with store staff and find out when they receive their shipment of plants from the nursery and, if possible, buy them on that exact day. This way you are spending your money on the healthiest plants possible that will give the best chance of success from the start. I would also encourage to buy as many plants as you can fit and afford in your aquarium. The more plants you have at the start, the healthier they are and the better you maintain them, the less likely you will suffer from algae.

EMERGED VS. SUBMERGED AQUATIC PLANTS

Plants in this shallow aquascape growing well above and below water.

In their natural habitats, the vast majority of aquatic plants will grow out of water (emerged) for much of their life and adapt to growing under water (submerged) during the rainy season when they become flooded. There are a handful of aquatic plants that *only* grow under water, with popular examples including *Vallisneria*, *Egeria*, and *Blyxa*. Most aquatic plants prefer to grow out of water because they have access to more light and CO_2 in the air, resulting in more robust and faster growth, as well as a greater ability to reproduce through their exposed flowers. Aquatic plants use

a lot of energy adapting from their emerged to submerged form, with many shedding their leaves completely (known as "melting" in the hobby) before new growth occurs, showing that they are readily adapted to their submerged form. Many species look completely different out of water, often characterized with more robust stems and leaves in their emerged state because they have to support their own weight in the air. When submerged, the plant is supported and often becomes more fragile. Leaves can also change shape and color considerably. When you buy your aquarium plant, it can be supplied in either form, emerged or submerged, or possibly in an in-between state.

Emerged plants travel much better, as they are physically more robust and aren't required to be 100 percent wet. The more fragile submerged plants can become damaged in transit and die off quickly if kept out of water for any significant length of time. Another disadvantage to submerged plants is that some species can struggle to adapt to an aquarium with differing water chemistry

The author pictured in one of the large greenhouses at Tropica Aquarium Plants in Denmark where plants are grown hydroponically.

to the supplier. Emerged plants, on the other hand, are more adaptable to a wider range of aquarium conditions and often fare better in transit. Some specialist aquarium stores will keep their aquarium plants in similar conditions to the greenhouses where they are grown emerged, giving you the healthiest plants possible.

However, the vast majority of retailers keep their plants under water in holding tanks. If you are lucky, the store will have good lighting, CO_2 injection, and good circulation in these systems to keep the plants healthy. The store will likely receive the vast majority of their plants from the greenhouses in their emerged state, then place them in their holding tank where hopefully they can adapt to their submerged state or sold on quickly before the plant starts adapting. As you can see, it can be a lottery whether you buy an emerged, submerged, or in-between plant. As a rule of thumb, most plants sold in bunches are already submerged and most plants sold in pots are originally emerged. The good news is that there are a group of plant products that take away this element of chance . . . enter the tissue-cultured aquarium plant.

TISSUE-CULTURED PLANTS: THE NEXT GENERATION OF AQUARIUM PLANT

My favorite aquarium plants are those that come supplied as tissue-cultured specimens.

These relatively young plants are grown in a special nutrient-rich liquid or gel in breathable yet water-tight containers. They're grown in sterile laboratory conditions and are therefore guaranteed to be free from algae, pest snails, pesticides, and disease. At first glance you may be put off due to their relatively small size, but don't let that fool you. There is actually a greater quantity of plants versus a regular pot. Because they're grown in a semi-aquatic environment with their liquid

Tissue-cultured plants represent the future of sustainable aquarium plant production.

growth media or gel, they immediately adapt to most aquarium conditions and begin growing right away. The speed at which most species grow is quite remarkable in my experience, even with lower lighting levels and no CO_2 injection. Because they are usually so small, they have delicate root structures and must be planted into your substrate using aquascaping tweezers. A soil-type substrate is best, with its loose structure and nutrient content which promotes root growth. They are effectively baby plants, so just like all babies they require regular feeding. Dose a good quality liquid fertilizer a couple of days after planting and keep a close eye on the growth. If there's any pale growth, then add more fertilizer. It is important to try to buy tissue-cultured plants in as good condition as possible. Unhealthy plants are usually obvious because the nutrient-rich growth liquid or gel is brown, and the plants look pale or brown. Avoid these and opt for plants with the cleanest looking growth media, whitest roots, and richest colors.

PRO TIP: WHAT TO LOOK FOR WHEN BUYING YOUR AQUARIUM PLANTS

1. Fresh-looking healthy leaves
2. Bright white roots (not translucent or brown)
3. No signs of algae
4. No signs of pest snails
5. No yellow or pale leaves
6. No holes or damaged leaves

PLANTS TO AVOID

The following plants are commonly sold as aquarium plants but are not suitable and will only grow out of water. They are often characterized with more color and variegated patterns when compared with most aquarium plants and have a more rigid structure. If in doubt, ask the store owner and if you are still not confident, then avoid an impulse purchase and research further. You can even use a plant ID app for your smart phone. I like "Plant Snap," which should identify all of these species with ease.

Acorus
Chlorophytum
Cordyline
Dracaena
Hemigraphis
Ophiopogon
Selaginella
Spathiphyllum
Syngonium
Trichomanes

POSITIONING YOUR PLANTS IN THE AQUASCAPE

If your aquarium is a canvas then the plants are the paint, so it is important to consider where they are positioned in order to give you the best overall impression. Plants grow to different sizes at different growth rates, so this also needs to be considered for the longer-term maintenance of your aquascape. Broadly speaking, we

Sumbersed vs. Emerged vs. Tissue-Cultured Plants

Plant Product	Pros	Cons
Submerged pot/bunch	Already adapted to underwater growth so can begin growing right away if aquarium conditions are suitable	Doesn't travel well so may be damaged upon receipt. Very prone to die-off if allowed to dry out
		May struggle to adapt to your aquarium conditions if they differ from the supplier
		More likely to be infested with pest snails and algae
		More likely to be treated with pesticides that can kill shrimp and snails
Emerged pot/bunch	Robust structure and travels very well	If kept for a long period in store may come supplied in a weakened condition with potential algae and pest snails
	More adaptable to a wider range of water parameters	Can struggle to adapt to your aquarium if supplied in a weakened condition - more likely to "melt"
	Less likely to become infested with pest snails and algae	
Tissue culture	Many more young plants supplied in each cup when compared with regular pot	Individual plants are smaller, so lack instant impact compared with more mature potted varieties
	Zero algae, pest snails, chance of disease or pesticides	Delicate root structure so can be challenging to plant. Aquascaping tweezers and soil substrate are recommended (not gravel).
	Will begin growing right away due it being adapted to semi-submerged growth	Can be more expensive vs regular pot (but usually less expensive per individual plant)
	Longer shelf life in store especially if kept at appropriate temperature (61°F/16°C)	
	Ships well due to being small and fully contained	

can split plants into four main categories for positioning in your aquarium: foreground, midground, background, and epiphyte. It is important to research your plants for each location in the aquascape in terms of their potential size to ensure they are appropriate in the long term. For example, you could by a small specimen of *Cryptocoryne crispatula* for your foreground, only to find it grows to over 18 in (45 cm) tall in a matter of a few weeks, therefore making it more suited to the background. Find out how tall your plant can eventually grow and consider if it suited to the height of your aquarium. Plants species are also available with different growth characteristics, i.e., carpeting, stem, rosette, rhizome, bulb, mosses, and floating.

Carpeting plants send out runners and new plants form at the end of these runners, i.e., *Glossostigma* and *Eleocharis*. This will eventually result in a full carpet effect across your aquascape. They are usually used in the foreground to create a solid lawn appearance that can look beautiful but often requires more lighting than other plants due to their lower position in the aquarium (where light has to penetrate further).

This *Helanthium tenellum* "Green" is a fast growing and easy carpeting plant.

Stem plants are formed from a stem with leaves growing outward from the stem. These are often the fastest growing plants, and thus require the most trimming. They are usually among the easiest species to propagate and are often used as background plants, i.e., *Limnophila* and *Rotala*. Red stem plants, such as *Ludwigia palustris*, are an ideal choice for creating high impact and focal points in your aquascape.

There are a huge variety of stem plants available representing all leaf shapes, sizes, and colors.

Rosette plants are formed from leaves that grow from a central root stock. They typically require lower maintenance and less trimming and are often best used

These *Cryptocoryne* species are a great example of easy to maintain rosette plants.

in the midground of your aquascape. My favorite rosette plants are *Cryptocoryne*. Some species such as *Echinodorus* can grow relatively tall so look best in the background. They usually have large root stocks and will benefit from a nutrient-rich substrate.

Rhizome plants are plants that grow their leaves from a rhizome, which is a fleshy portion of the plants where the leaves and roots grow from. They are typically epiphyte plants that should be attached to your hardscape, i.e., *Anubias*, *Microsorum*, and *Bucephalandra*. They are a great choice for adding a sense of maturity to the aquascape from the outset and should be positioned carefully on your hardscape to give the best aesthetic balance possible. Because their roots are not in the substrate, they obtain their required nutrients from the aquarium water.

The beautiful *Bucephalandra* growing as an epihypte on these aquarium rocks add a great sense of maturity.

Bulb plants are often used as solitary specimens to create a high impact focal point in the aquascape, i.e., *Nymphaea lotus*. The leaves and roots grow from the bulb that contains a lot of nutrients, although they will benefit from a nutrient-rich substrate. The bulb is usually best planted just underneath the substrate surface with the exposed leaves just above the substrate to allow for light to reach them.

Nymphaea lotus is a popular and fast growing tropical lily bulb plant.

Mosses look great attached to wood or rocks. They are usually a slow grower and should be initially attached using only thin layers. If a too large clump of moss is attached, then the lower layers become starved of light and circulating water which can cause die-off. Regular trimming promotes fresh and compact new growth moss. It is a good idea to have a population of shrimp in an aquascape with moss, as they constantly graze it for biofilm and algae that can otherwise soon build up and look unsightly.

The roots of floating plants offer shelter and security to many aquarium fish species.

Floating plants are among the fastest growing species due to their location nearest the light source and access to CO_2 in the air. Because they are the fastest growers, they are often the first to show any nutrient deficiencies with pale growth. This is an indication that more liquid fertilizers may be required. Regular thinning out of floating plants will be required in order to prevent them from overshadowing the other plants in the aquarium. Some species such as *Limnobium laevigatum* have long dangling roots that provide additional shelter and security for your fish.

HOW TO PREPARE YOUR PLANTS
POTTED PLANTS

1. Remove the entire plant from the pot.
2. Split the rockwool (fiberglass growing media) into two halves and remove as much of it as possible from the root stock. You can do this under water with aquascaping tweezers to make it easier.
3. Carefully divide the plant mass into as many individual plants as possible by splitting apart with your fingers.
4. Trim the roots back to approximately 1 in (2 cm) with aquascaping scissors.

5. Plant into your substrate using aquascaping tweezers. Ensure the roots are covered by the substrate to provide sufficient anchorage.

TISSUE-CULTURE PLANTS

1. Remove the pot lid.
2. Remove the plant mass from the pot.
3. Using a bowl of tepid water, rinse off the growth media from the plants.
4. Split the plant mass into as many portions as possible.
5. Plant into your substrate using aquascaping tweezers. Ensure the roots are covered by the substrate to provide sufficient anchorage.

HOW TO ATTACH EPIPHYTE PLANTS

There are three main ways to attach epiphyte plants. The quickest and easiest method is to simply wedge the plant into a gap in the hardscape if possible. I often like to insert plants like *Anubias* between wood and rocks where it will often be shaded (*Anubias* grows well in the shade). Another popular method is to use a cyanoacrylate-based gel glue (superglue). Simply dab a tiny amount of the glue onto the desired spot on the hardscape and press the plant gently against it for a few seconds. This needs to be done out of water. Gel-type superglue is best because it doesn't run, which will create a distracting bright white marking. Be careful not to glue your fingers during this process! Another popular method, but more labor intensive, is to tie the plants onto the hardscape with cotton thread or fishing line.

MAINTAINING AND PROPAGATING AQUARIUM PLANTS

At some point you will need to maintain your aquarium plants. They will need trimming when they become overgrown and these trimmings can also be used to propagate some species of plant. Overgrown plants will make the aquascape look chaotic but can also lead to poor circulation around the whole aquarium. Plants also need maintaining in order to keep them looking fresh and to promote new growth. A good example of this is to simply remove any unhealthy leaves from an otherwise healthy plant, as this will encourage fresh and healthy growth. It is better for the plant to spend its energy on growing new leaves than wasting energy trying to repair a damaged leaf. The same principle can be applied to leaves infested with algae; remove these to encourage new growth (that can fight off algae).

MAINTAINING CARPETING PLANTS

Most carpeting species will eventually require thinning out as the plants grow on top of each other leading to the bottom plants becoming starved of light and circulating water. These lower plants can die off, leading to a build-up of waste organics and algae. Using curved scissors is a popular method to trim the carpet and the floating off-cuts can be netted off from the aquarium surface. With severely overgrown carpets you can remove the entire carpet in one go, as the plants are often matted together. Then simply divide the carpet into as many individual plants as required and re-plant with aquascaping tweezers.

Trimming stem plants can be important to maintain visual balance in your aquascape.

Trimming stem plants is necessary to keep them from becoming too tall and to maintain the overall aesthetic of your aquascape. It's important to note that the majority of stem plants will grow two new shoots from the point where you trimmed, and this can be useful to encourage a dense bushy effect. For this reason, it is also important to be mindful where you trim the stem. After several trimming sessions, one single stem can have many stems branching out above. This lower stem then becomes starved of light, potentially losing their leaves as the uppermost stems thrive. At this point it is a good idea to trim off the healthy growing stems and re-plant and uproot the less attractive lower stems and discard. Stem plant maintenance is an art in itself, and is something I am still learning to this day!

MAINTAINING ROSETTE, BULB, AND EPIPHYTE PLANTS
Rosette, bulb, and epiphyte plants are relatively easy to maintain when compared with carpets and stems. Simply remove any leaves that are too large or look unhealthy. Try to remove the leaf directly from the rootstock by pulling or peeling it away if possible, as this will encourage new leaf growth. Rhizomes from epiphyte plants can be split and re-attached elsewhere in order to propagate them. Some rosette plants can also form runners that can be trimmed off or re-planted for propagation.

MAINTAINING MOSS
Trim off any excess moss growth with aquascaping scissors and siphon out the cuttings to prevent them from sinking and potentially growing elsewhere in the aquarium. Cuttings can easily be propagated by re-attaching on your hardscape.

CHAPTER NINE
HOW TO CHOOSE YOUR FISH, SHRIMP, AND SNAILS

Stocking your aquarium with fish, shrimp, and snails is one of the most exciting parts of the entire aquascaping process. For me, they are the vital ingredients that can provide the perfect balance of movement, color, and behavior to really bring an aquascape to life. With hundreds of species to choose from, there are plenty of suitable (and unsuitable) candidates. The main priority should always be the welfare of the animal. Make sure to do research so as to ensure your aquarium water chemistry, temperature, and overall setup are compatible with any livestock you wish to keep. For example, soft water, shade-loving fish shouldn't be kept in a hard water Iwagumi aquascapes with open space and bright lighting. Ideally, the water chemistry of your aquarium will match or be close to the supplier. Most captive-bred fish are adaptable to a wide range of parameters, but always do your research before purchasing livestock. Impulse buys, however tempting, should be avoided, just as you wouldn't rush out and buy any pet on a whim (I hope!). You can split your livestock up into two broad categories, although they aren't mutually exclusive: display and maintenance. Your display fish should be chosen to compliment the aquarium and aquascape from an aesthetic viewpoint.

Large shoals of a single species of small fish are a great way to add a sense of scale and create a more natural feel to the aquascape.

It's also important to note whether your potential fish choice will either eat or dig up your plants, so it's usually best to avoid herbivorous or particularly boisterous fish. Any maintenance livestock can be added to help deal with background levels of algae (Amano shrimp and Nerite snails are great examples) and other tasks such as keeping the substrate aerated in the case of Malaysian trumpet snails. It's important not to rely on algae-eating fish and shrimp to cure an already algae infested aquarium unless the underlying cause of the algae is identified and remedied.

SIZE MATTERS
Tank size is an essential consideration, and always make sure to stock it assuming the potential full size of the fish and not the current size when purchased (as fish are often sold as juveniles). Stocking guidelines are

Small, shallow aquascapes are best suited to small and slender fish.

Aquariums with a taller aspect ratio suit taller-bodied fish.

not an exact science due to there being so many variables, such as filtration capacity, water change schedule, aquarium temperature, and plant growth. My personal taste is on the side of "less is more," and I often keep far fewer fish than I could.

Just because you *could* fit more fish in your tank doesn't mean you *should*. Fewer fish results in less waste, less required maintenance, and a lower risk of algae. Also consider the visual balance between the plants, hardscape, and fish. For instance, you may have a tranquil aquascape design that could be thrown off by having too many highly active and distracting fish. Consider the aquarium dimensions in terms of its height and length; known as the aspect ratio. Taller tanks suit taller-bodied fish and shallower tanks more streamline species. Always ensure there is plenty of swimming space—especially for fish that originate from fast-flowing water. Also, take into account where the fish naturally likes to swim in the aquarium space, i.e., top, middle, or bottom dwellers. Allow this swimming pattern to complement your aquascape design. For example, an aquarium with a lot of open sand space would suit a large shoal of Cory catfish (*Corydorus*), but a large densely planted jungle style aquascape with tall plants may be more suited to angelfish (*Pterophyllum scalare*). Try to make your fish selection match your aquascape so the whole effect is one of coherence and harmony that not only looks great but, more importantly, suits the needs of the fish and promotes their natural behavior. Aquascapes also tend to look more natural with larger shoals of smaller fish. The sense of scale looks more impressive with small fish, especially in smaller aquariums. It can also be so impactful and relaxing to see a huge aquarium with literally hundreds of small schooling fish, where their behavior is going to be more natural. Smaller fish produce proportionately much

Discus are often considered the king of the freshwater aquarium and given the right conditions
will spawn regularly.

less waste than larger fish, too. For example, ten 1 in (2.5 cm) fish produce less waste than one 10 in (20 cm) fish. Larger fish that are kept as single specimens, pairs, or small groups can also look great in larger aquariums but can overwhelm a smaller aquarium—both aesthetically and biologically. Some popular larger fish that do well in larger groups include discus and angelfish, with a well-planted discus aquarium being considered the pinnacle of freshwater fishkeeping by many.

PRO TIP: BE PATIENT!

Don't stock your aquascape with display fish until the aquarium is showing healthy plant growth and is beginning to take shape in terms of how you visualize your end goal. During these initial few weeks, be patient and use the time to research potential display fish candidates. However, stocking your maintenance livestock—such as with shrimp and snails—is a good idea from the start to help prevent algae.

SPECIES SHORTLIST

There are far too many fish, shrimp, and snail species to list, but here are a few tried-and-tested species that are suitable for most sizes of aquascape. Remember: always do your research before buying any livestock to ensure they will be compatible with your water chemistry and other aquarium inhabitants.

FISH

These golden barbs are an active and colorful fish suitable for unheated aquascapes.

Green neon rasboras are small enough to be kept in nano aquascapes, adding a subtle yet beautiful hint of green.

The Green neon tetra shows the best color when kept in a densely planted aquarium.

The popular and tiny celestial pearl danio can be quite shy so provide plenty of surface cover to keep them comfortable.

My favorite fish for aquascaping include tetras, rasboras, danios, minnows, and barbs, as most of these species stay small, giving a great sense of scale when kept in larger shoals. They are usually very peaceful (with the odd exception—do your research!), and with so many species to choose from there is virtually every color and shape available to match all tastes and aquascapes. Other suitable smaller fish include dwarf cichlids such as *Apistogramma* and bottom-dwelling fish such as Cory catfish.

Apistogramma are a stunning fish that are often kept in pairs to obtain maximum coloration.

In my experience, it is better to stick with fewer species but keep them in greater numbers, as this looks more natural. In larger aquariums, you can carry on

Pearl gouramis can look great in larger aquascapes. But beware, as they may predate on small shrimp.

with stocking smaller species but have many more fish in your shoals. If you decide to stock larger fish, ensure they complement the aquascape and won't present a predatory risk to any small fish or shrimp you already keep or plan to own.

SHRIMP

Amano shrimp are a hugely popular and hardy algae eater for many aquascapes.

Cherry shrimp can breed prolifically in most aquascapes providing they aren't threatened by fish.

Bee shrimp require more specific water parameters than Amano and cherry shrimp.

There are dozens of freshwater shrimp species available, but the most commonly available and suitable for aquascaping include Amano shrimp (*Caridina multidentata*), Cherry shrimp (*Neocaridina davidi*), and

Bee shrimp (*Caridina cf. cantonensis*). Amano shrimp are well known for their algae-eating function and do not breed in freshwater. Cherry shrimp and the huge variety of color morphs are colorful and easy to breed. They don't eat algae as efficiently as Amano shrimp, but constantly graze all the plants and hardscape surfaces for biofilm, which can help prevent algae. Bee shrimp and their varieties are more sensitive than Amano and cherry shrimp and usually do best in softer water, ideally made from re-mineralized reverse osmosis (RO) filtered water. They will breed in the right conditions but do so best in aquariums dedicated to them with no fish present. Shrimp are perfect for nano aquariums where you are forced to look closely and appreciate them. Consider a shrimp-only setup, as this will allow them to exhibit their most natural behavior without fear of predation from any fish.

SNAILS

Snails can be both desirable and regarded as pests depending on the species and your own taste. Most eat algae, leftover fish food, detritus, and biofilm, which can make them a helpful addition, although some species breed so easily and prolifically that an overpopulation can spoil the look of your aquascape. Only a few species will eat healthy plants, as they prefer decaying matter and algae. Desirable species include nerite snails: Zebra nerite (*Neritina natalensis)*, Tiger nerite (*Vittina semiconica*), and Horned nerite (*Clithon corona/diadema*).

A shrimp-only aquascape is a great way to observe their most natural behavior.

Nerite snails are great a way to keep stubborn algae growth on wood and rocks under control.

Bladder snails are considered a pest by most with their asexual reproduction resulting in populations than can grow out of control.

These look attractive and are great algae eaters that do not breed in freshwater. Some can lay stubborn white eggs that can look unsightly, but my personal preference is to see these over algae. They are particularly good at grazing the stubborn algae that most fish and shrimp do not touch.

Another popular snail species is the Malaysian trumpet snail (*Melanoides tuberculata*), although they are regarded as a pest by many. These species eat algae and leftover food, and also help to keep the substrate turned over—but will breed prolifically in most aquariums.

Regarded as a pest snail by almost everyone is the bladder snail (*Physa acuta*).

Although they do eat algae, waste food, biofilm, and detritus, their rapid rate of reproduction can look unsightly, with literally hundreds of snails soon crawling all over your aquascape. It's a similar story with Ramshorn snails (*Planorbarius corneus* and *Planorbella duryi*), although some hobbyists find these more desirable with some colorful and relatively large varieties available.

PRO TIP: CHOOSE YOUR FISH CAREFULLY

Try to avoid creating a "Noah's Ark" aquarium. It's tempting to stock your aquarium with a diverse range of species, but this can look incoherent and unnatural. Most shoaling species do best in groups of at least ten, and the more the better. The most stunning larger aquascapes can feature literally hundreds of the same species. The effect of one tight shoal swimming up and down the aquarium is truly wonderful. Don't stock fish that will eat or dig up plants. If in doubt, do your research.

Ramshorn snails can breed prolifically in most planted aquariums.

My stepson, Harrison, performing maintenance duties by cleaning the aquarium glass.

CHAPTER TEN
MAINTENANCE

One of the most important points to get across in this book is the importance of regular and appropriate maintenance. An aquascape will only provide you with a pleasurable viewing experience if it is maintained at the right time and in the right way. Just how often and how much maintenance depends largely on the type of system you have. For example, a high-energy aquascape with high levels of lighting, nutrients, and fast-growing plants will require proportionately more maintenance than a low-energy aquarium with slow-growing plants and low lighting. The larger your aquarium, the more time it will usually take to maintain—especially when it comes to the all-important water changes.

Siphoning out old aquarium water with a hose directly into the garden is a great way to recycle the nutrient-rich water.

PREVENTATIVE VS. CORRECTIVE MAINTENANCE

You may have heard of the phrase "Prevention is better than cure," and this is most definitely the case when it comes to maintaining aquascapes. The most common issue you will experience in your aquarium is algae, and it will soon rear its ugly head if maintenance is neglected. Once you have algae, it can take a lot of time and energy to clear it up. It is, therefore, much better to

> **PRO TIP: MICRO MAINTENANCE**
>
> Try to situate your aquarium where you will be viewing it regularly. This will help provide the trigger and motivation to want to maintain your aquascape, as you will be constantly reminded of its current state. I have my largest aquascape just a few feet away from my home office desk, where I spend much of my working day. This provides a welcome view when I have the opportunity to relax for a few minutes or I'm on a call. I often use this opportunity to execute "micro maintenance" sessions, such as the removal of a dead leaf or quick trimming of a stem plant. These micro sessions add up over the week and make the larger planned weekly maintenance tasks quicker and easier. This process also gives me the opportunity to consider what larger maintenance tasks require undertaking during the scheduled weekly session.

maintain your aquarium as frequently as necessary to prevent algae from occurring in the first place. Knowing what maintenance to carry out and how often can be a challenge for beginners, but by following this simple guide you should be able to prevent the vast majority of issues from occurring; from poor plant growth and algae outbreaks to cloudy water and fish disease.

MAINTENANCE SCHEDULES

It is a great idea to schedule a specific day (or days) of the week for your aquarium maintenance. Try to allow at least one maintenance session of one hour per week, and a few minutes every day. Try to make this time non-negotiable; let your family know—or even encourage them to help—and allow it to form a part of your routine. Over time it should become a habit and something you look forward to. Try not to think about maintenance as a chore but as an opportunity to constantly improve your aquascape.

Suggested Schedules and Maintenance Activities
Daily

- **Check Aquarium Water Level**: Ensure that there is no leaking or excessive evaporation, which can cause a build-up of mineral content in the aquarium water.
- **Check Filter Operation:** A visual check to see if water is flowing sufficiently from the filter outlet.
- **Check Water Temperature**: A thermometer is ideal to monitor temperature. Ensure the temperature is appropriate for your livestock.

- **Check CO_2 is Operational if CO_2 Injection is Being Used**: A visual check of the bubble counter or diffuser is usually sufficient. Also check contents of cylinder if you are running a pressurized system.
- **Feed the Fish**: This is the perfect time to also check on your fish health.
- **Check Condition of Plants and Inspect for Algae:** Inspect for pale or yellowing of leaves and algae so you're aware as to the health of your aquarium.
- **Add Liquid Fertilizer:** Dose the appropriate quantity of liquid fertilizer.

Invest in a good quality glass cleaning sponge and it will save you a lot of effort.

Weekly

- **Clean Aquarium Glass:** Use an algae sponge or magnet. A toothbrush and credit card (or similar) are also useful to clean in any hard-to-reach areas, such as the corners and area near the substrate.
- **Clean Filter:** Depending on the amount of waste produced, filtration type, and media, you can do this less frequently. Clean any biological media in old aquarium water to avoid killing beneficial bacteria. If you are using an external filter, then the hoses, and filter inlet and outlets may need cleaning with a hose brush.
- **Trim Excess Plant Growth:** Use sharp aquascaping scissors to trim any overgrown plants. Re-plant trimmings, give them away, or dispose of carefully. Note: Do not allow them to enter natural waterways!
- **Siphon Loose Organic Waste Accumulation from Substrate:** This is best done as part of the water change. I gently wave my hand just above the substrate to lift up any collected detritus and siphon away during the water removal.
- **Water Change:** In most circumstances, I recommend a 50 percent per week water change. Ensure the water change is carried out as the very last part of the maintenance process. This helps to remove the waste organics and algae that you have dislodged into the aquarium water, therefore helping to prevent further algae.

THE IMPORTANCE OF WATER CHANGES

In my experience, the most important maintenance practice for the vast majority of aquascapes is the water change. The aquarium is a closed system, where any waste is allowed to accumulate. We usually have a filter and plant growth to prevent the waste from becoming acutely toxic to any livestock, but over time waste organics and oxygen-consuming "bad" bacteria are certain to build up. This may eventually lead to an array of issues, from stunted fish growth to algae. The water change is a simple and effective way to help prevent this by diluting this waste organic-laden stale water by replenishing with fresh water. This regular dilution of waste and replenishing with fresh water keeps your aquarium healthy, resulting in more vibrant fish, shrimp, and plants, plus less algae. In my experience, there is an undeniable correlation between the frequency and amount of water being changed with the overall vitality of the entire aquarium system, providing, of course, that the supplied water is suitable.

How to Perform a Water Change

There are many ways to change water, and the best method will be dependent on your own circumstances—such as the size of the aquarium, where it is located in relation to your water supply, and if you are using mains supply water or pre-prepared water (i.e., reverse osmosis or de-ionized water). The simplest method and one I used for many years was with a 3-gal (12-L) bucket and length of hose. One end of the hose goes into the aquarium and the other is used to siphon into the bucket. You can imagine how long it took me to perform a 50 percent water change of a 100-gal (400-L) aquarium—not to mention the chronic lower back pain!

Now I use a much less labor-intensive method that saves me time, energy, and lower back pain. It assumes you have access to a hot and cold water tap and sink that's large enough to house a bucket. Please note this method is suited to larger aquariums. I still use the basic bucket and hose method for aquariums under 15 gal (60 L). I recommend experimenting and developing your own techniques as required. It is important that your water change method works well for you, as you will be doing a great deal of them during your time in the hobby!

Kit Needed

My aquascape maintenance kit.

A dedicated tool kit is a great idea to keep frequently used items to hand.

- Length of hose: long enough to reach from sink to aquarium and from aquarium to outside or toilet. Diameter of hose needs to fit onto submergible pump. I use a hose with 16 mm internal diameter.
- Submergible pump: I use an Eheim Compact 1000.
- Bucket: 3 gal (12 L)
- Spare external filter inlet (16 mm diameter)

SUGGESTED MAINTENANCE KIT

- Aquarium-only use bucket
- Syphon hose
- Aquarium-only toothbrush
- Old credit card or similar item
- Algae wiping sponge or magnet
- Aquascaping tweezers
- Aquascaping scissors
- Flexible hose brush
- Kitchen colander (in red, if possible)
- De-chlorinator
- Fish net
- Towels
- Aquarium-safe glass cleaner

HOW TO REMOVE OLD AQUARIUM WATER

1. Place spare external filter inlet inside aquarium so the inlet strainer portion is at least halfway down into the aquarium water.
2. Attach one end of hose to the external filter inlet and have the other end of the hose running outside (or another location) to allow the waste aquarium water to flow. I like to water the plants in my garden with my wastewater.
3. Start the siphon by sucking on the free end of the hose. One sharp and purposeful suck should start the siphon easily with no risk of accidentally ingesting waste aquarium water!
4. Drain as much water from your aquarium as required. I recommend 50 percent for most circumstances. During this process you should use the opportunity to undertake other maintenance tasks, such as cleaning the glass and siphoning waste organics from the substrate. The idea as that any dislodged waste matter will be removed during the water change, therefore helping to reduce the risk of algae and giving you cleaner water.

HOW TO ADD FRESH WATER

Using a kitchen colander is a great way to disperse the added fresh water, preventing it from disturbing the substrate.

1. Set up your submergible pump in the bottom of your bucket in your sink.
2. Fill the bucket with water at the correct temperature to match your aquarium water. While your tank temperature may vary, for mine I use a mixture of hot and cold together to obtain approximately 75°F/24°C.
3. Attach the free end of the hose to the submergible pump.
4. You may wish to move the end of the hose that's in the aquarium to a position where the freshwater outflow won't excessively disturb the substrate or plants. I like to use a kitchen colander.
5. Turn on the pump and simultaneously have your fresh water filling the bucket at the same rate the water is being pumped into your aquarium. This may take some adjusting to reach the right balance.
6. Add dechlorinator to the aquarium during the process. I add a half dose at the start of the filling process then another half dose at the end.
7. Fill the aquarium up to the desired level, keeping an eye on the bucket to ensure it doesn't run empty, which can damage the pump. Better to have the bucket overflow into the sink than your floor.

WATER CHEMISTRY AND TEST KITS

Water chemistry is a complex topic, but the good news is that by focusing on creating a well-maintained aquarium environment suitable for plant growth, you do need to be overly concerned with water chemistry or testing. However, it can be helpful to know if you have hard or soft water from your main supply, as this can determine which fish and invertebrates are most likely to thrive in your aquarium. A basic test kit for pH (the water acidity or alkalinity), KH (carbonate hardness), and GH (general hardness) will give you an idea. Electronic devices that measure totally dissolved solids (TDS) or conductivity are also relatively affordable and much easier to use and read. As a basic guideline, the lower the pH and hardness/TDS/conductive, the softer your water will be, and vice-versa. If you are keeping mostly captive-bred fish and shrimp, then it is a good idea to buy them from a supplier that has similar water chemistry to your own. Wild-caught fish and sensitive shrimp may require more specific water conditions—such as very soft and acidic water—so do you research and match your aquarium water appropriately. Some water supplies can be very high in nitrates and phosphates, which may cause issues with algae in non-planted or sparsely planted aquariums. In healthy aquariums with plenty of plant growth, these nitrates and phosphates will happily be used to help plant growth that, in turn, will help prevent algae. This is another great reason why you should consider a densely planted aquarium!

REVERSE OSMOSIS WATER

If your main water supply is particularly unsuitable for the livestock you intend to keep, then the best option is to use reverse osmosis (RO) water. This is water that has been passed through a special filter that removes all the minerals resulting in pure water. This is usually unsuitable for the aquarium if used directly, so commercially available minerals need to be re-added. The amount added is determined by the water chemistry you are aiming for, and this is where a TDS or conductivity meter is helpful. You can buy RO water from an aquarium store or make your own using an RO unit that is plumbed into your mains water supply. I do not personally use RO water, as I find my hard tap water perfectly fine to keep my chosen fish, shrimp, and plants. However, if I wished to breed specific fish or shrimp, or grow very delicate plants to their best potential, then an RO unit would be a consideration.

IS REVERSE OSMOSIS WATER WORTH IT?

The vast majority of plants have the ability to adapt to hard or soft water. I have experienced slightly improved growth with some plant species in softer water, but not enough to justify me using RO water. For me, the amount of extra time, energy, and expense that's required to use RO water and the necessary re-mineralization is not a justifiable trade-off in any plant growth improvement.

It is my hope that you do not underestimate the importance of establishing a good maintenance practice in your aquascape. An aquascape and the plants will only look good if they are maintained appropriately. Try to make your (at least) weekly maintenance time non-negotiable and set aside a specific day and time. If you can learn to enjoy the maintenance tasks

this is also hugely beneficial—I like to listen to music (electronic) or my favorite podcasts (usually bio-hacking related) during my sessions. If you perceive it to be a chore, then you are more likely to find an excuse not to do it. Consider the longer-term rewards of being diligent and consistent, and your aquascape, the plants, and the livestock will thank you for it—but algae will not!

ALGAE: AVOIDING AND TROUBLESHOOTING

No book on aquariums and aquascaping would be complete without a section dedicated to algae. I still suffer with it occasionally, and probably always will due to inevitable periods of neglect on my home aquariums with my busy travel schedule. (Author's note: At the time of writing we are experiencing the global coronavirus pandemic and traveling is restricted. My home aquascapes have never been so well-maintained!) Although I can count on my family members to perform basic tasks, such as feeding the fish and adding a liquid fertilizer, it's perhaps a step too far to ask them to perform 50 percent water changes on six aquariums! Thankfully, I can soon get the tanks back on track after experiencing any algae issues by diligently changing water, focusing on healthy plant growth, and performing the other necessary maintenance tasks.

Algae issues are stated to be the number one reason aquarium owners decide to give up on their hobby. They have potentially invested a lot of time and money into their aquariums only to struggle with algae, leaving them with a bad experience and sometimes preventing them from having another aquarium. The good news is that, by following the advice in this book, you can prevent algae from occurring . . . or at least manage it and treat it so it doesn't return to the point where you want to give up. There are literally thousands of algae species and it's one of the oldest life forms on this planet. For this reason, it is very adaptable to a wide range of conditions and, given the opportunity, will almost definitely rear its ugly head in your aquarium.

PREVENTING ALGAE

The key to success in dealing with any algae is to prevent it by focusing on healthy plant growth in combination with appropriate maintenance practices. I like to think of algae and aquarium plants as being in a constant battle with each other. Algae always has the potential to infest your aquarium if your plants aren't cared for and your tank isn't well maintained. The more plants you have, the healthier they are and the better maintained your aquarium is as a whole, with less risk of algae. We have already discussed maintenance practices, such as water changes, filter cleaning, and substrate maintenance—these are all essential to avoid the accumulation of waste organic matter, which is one of the biggest triggers of algae.

Here is a list of factors that will encourage algae and what you can do to help prevent it.

1. Too Much Light

If you have a lot of light—both intensity and duration—but not the right amount of plants and plant growth to be able to utilize this light, then algae will be the result. Aim to use enough light to grow your most demanding plants, but not much more. Stick to a photoperiod of no longer than 8 hours and use a plug-in timer to ensure consistency. Plant densely with a proportion of fast-growing species and consider floating plants—especially in the early weeks after initial set up, such as *Hygrophila* and *Salvinia*.

2. Not Enough Water Changes

If you do not make sufficient water changes, then waste organics will build in your tank, which will trigger algae. Change at least 50 percent of your aquarium water every week to dilute the waste organics and reset the nutrient levels provided by your regular liquid fertilizer addition.

3. Stale Substrates

If there is a large accumulation of waste in the substrate and not enough plant growth to deal with it, then algae will happily utilize this organic waste build-up. Remove the excess accumulation of waste from your substrate during your regular water changes by gently waving your hand near the substrate surface and siphoning out the lifted detritus.

4. Dirty Filters

Excessively dirty filters that are clogged with waste will trigger algae due to the consequent poor flow and circulation that lead to dead spots in the aquarium. This will lead to poor plant growth, giving algae the upper hand. Clean your filter media regularly as part of your scheduled maintenance program.

5. Too Many Fish and Overfeeding

Fish produce a lot of waste organics that will lead to algae unless this waste is dealt with by a combination of healthy plant growth and good maintenance practices. Better to deliberately understock your aquarium with smaller fish and feed them little and often. Consider stocking a larger proportion of algae-eating shrimp instead of algae-eating fish, as their waste production and requirement for additional food is considerably lower.

6. High Temperatures

All aquarium metabolic processes are determined by the temperature of the water. The warmer the water the more waste is produced and the less oxygen is present. Low oxygen levels result in less efficient beneficial bacteria processes and a quicker production of algae-triggering waste organics. If possible, run your aquarium on the cooler side, but always consider the welfare of your fish. Research the lowest temperature at which your livestock will comfortably thrive and aim for that.

ALGAE TYPES AND TREATMENTS

There are too many algae species to describe in detail in this book, but the good news is that they can all be prevented in the same manner as described above. Treating algae is a more complex topic, and effective remedies largely depend on the type of algae. I have listed the four most common groups of algae below.

Cyanobacteria

This is actually a photosynthetic bacteria rather than algae. It's commonly known as blue green algae (BGA) or slime algae due to its appearance. It also has a distinctive foul smell and can rapidly cover the entire aquarium if not dealt with quickly. It is usually caused by a build-up of organic waste in conjunction with poor circulation and excess light. It originates in the substrate and can often be triggered by sunlight or bright ambient light hitting the aquarium glass at the substrate level.

Treatment of Cyanobacteria

1. Manually remove as much as possible by siphoning out during a large water change. Really pay attention to getting rid of every last visible part. Any tiny leftovers can quickly take hold again.

2. Perform a 72-hour complete blackout by covering all of your aquarium with newspaper/ blocking out any natural light that may hit your tank and turning off your lights.

3. During the blackout, turn off your CO_2 injection (if applicable) and have your filter outlet agitating the water surface to boost oxygen levels. Avoid peeking, and do not feed your fish during this period. Because cyanobacteria is a photosynthetic bacteria, it will die off without direct light.

4. After the 72 hours, remove the aquarium

covers. All traces of the cyanobacteria should have disappeared.

5. Perform a large water change, paying attention to siphoning around the substrate and previously infected plants.

6. Clean your filter.

7. Address the cause of the cyanobacteria to prevent it from reoccurring. Consider more plants and circulation levels, along with more frequent water changes and substrate maintenance. Take measures to limit any excess ambient light from hitting the aquarium glass at the substrate level.

Black Brush/Beard Algae (BBA)

BBA is one of the most common and stubborn types of algae that you can experience in an established planted aquarium. It is characterized by fine hairy black or brown filaments that resemble a brush or beard, hence

The dreaded black brush algae (BBA) is one of the most challenging forms of algae.

its name. As with other algae types, it's typically caused by excess waste organic accumulation and is often found growing on wood, presumably attracted by any leeching organics. It is also prone to grow on any slow-growing plant species that are not healthy. BBA is also known to be triggered by fluctuating CO_2 levels that are often associated with poor CO_2 injection management.

Treatment of BBA

Manual removal of BBA can be challenging due to its stubborn nature, so an effective technique can be to spot treat a glutaraldehyde-based or hydrogen peroxide product. There are aquarium products marketed as liquid carbon fertilizers that contain glutaraldehyde, usually diluted to around 2 percent active ingredient.

1. Drain your aquarium water to expose the BBA. If the BBA is at the bottom of the tank, then you may need to move the infected piece out of the aquarium and treat externally.

2. Carefully pour a small quantity of your glutaraldehyde or hydrogen peroxide–based product into a small container.

3. Use a small artist's paintbrush to "paint" the product directly onto the BBA and allow to soak in for a few minutes.

4. Fill up the aquarium with fresh water or replace the infected piece back into the tank.

5. Carry out a 50 percent water change.

6. The BBA should turn a white or purple color within 48 hours and disappear within a week.
7. Address the cause of your BBA to prevent it from reoccurring by focusing on overall aquarium cleanliness, ideal CO_2 injection management (if used) and plant health.

Green Dust Algae (GDA)

GDA is a relatively common algae that shows up on aquarium glass, but not usually so much on the hardscape or plants. It's a frustrating algae, as it spoils the view of your aquascape and even after a thorough cleaning of the glass it can become covered with the green dust algae again a day or so later. It's typically caused by a sudden fluctuation in nutrient levels (especially a spike in nitrogen) and/or lighting. Its treatment is very straight forward, yet requires some patience.

1. Simply allow the GDA to build up on the glass or any other surface for three to four weeks without cleaning it. This allows the algae spores to go through their entire lifecycle.
2. Thoroughly clean all affected surfaces.
3. Perform a large water change—ideally at least 75 percent.
4. Clean your filter.
5. Ensure your lighting is appropriate both in its intensity and photoperiod.
6. Address the cause of your GDA to prevent it from reoccurring by focusing on overall aquarium cleanliness, ideal nutrient management (such as daily fertilizer dosing), and plant health.

Hair Algae

Green hair algae is usually associated with an imbalance of light and nutrients.

Staghorn algae usually attaches itself to the weakest part of the plant.

This diverse range of algae species includes types commonly known as staghorn algae, green hair algae, green fluff algae, and filamentous algae. They can all be prevented and treated in a similar manner and are usually caused by an accumulation of organic waste in conjunction with too much light, poor nutrient dosing, and poor plant health.

1. Manually remove as much of the algae as possible.
2. Trim off any severely affected leaves to allow new and healthy growth.
3. Carry out a large water change to dilute any dislodged floating algae particles.
4. Clean your filter.
5. Ensure your lighting is appropriate.
6. Address the cause of your hair algae to prevent it from reoccurring by focusing on overall aquarium cleanliness, ideal nutrient and CO_2 management, and plant health.

Brown Algae

Brown algae, also known as diatoms, are usually only associated with new aquariums and is very easy to remove manually or by adding algae-eating fish, shrimp, and snails. If you are patient enough, most diatoms will actually disappear themselves after the aquarium has become established with enough healthy plant growth and beneficial bacteria. I have found that I can prevent diatoms from occurring by performing large frequent water changes for the first month weeks

Brown algae or diatoms is very common in new aquascapes and will usually disappear on its own if regular maintenance is carried out.

after initial set up, and by adding a suitable algae-eating crew after the first 2 to 3 weeks.

Algae-Eating Fish and Shrimp

I've deliberately left mentioning algae-eating fish and shrimp for the end of this section on algae. All too often, I find many hobbyists' first thought when it comes to solving their algae issues is to add fish that eat the algae. This can be helpful, but unless the cause of the algae is addressed then it will return, and any amount of algae eating fish or shrimp is unlikely to provide a long-term solution. It is always better to focus on healthy plant health and good aquarium maintenance before even considering your algae crew, as this will give you the best chance of keeping your aquarium free from algae problems. That said, adding an algae crew is a great idea to help keep down background levels of algae that will occur naturally, even in a well-maintained aquascape

Amano shrimp

Nerite snail

Cherry shrimp

full of healthy plants. My preference is to use a combination of Amano shrimp (*Cardinia multidentata)*, Cherry shrimp (*Neocardinia davidii*), and Nerite snails (*Neritana natalensis*).

The best defense against algae is healthy plant growth and lots of it!

PRO TIP: ALGAE CREW STOCKING RECOMMENDATIONS

Amano shrimp: 1 shrimp per 2 gal (8 L) of aquarium water.

Cherry shrimp: 1 shrimp per 1 gal (4 L) of aquarium water.

Nerite snail: 1 snail per 3 gal (12 L) of aquarium water.

I tend not to use fish as algae eaters, but a popular choice are otos (*Otocinclus*) species for smaller aquariums and Siamese algae eaters (*Crossocheilus siamensis*) for larger aquariums. In my experience, shrimp and snails provide a better algae-eating solution versus how much waste they produce when compared with fish.

My friends Jurijs Jutjajevs and Michael Mikkelsen relaxing in front of Michael's beautiful aquascape.

CONCLUSION

Aquascaping is one of the most beautiful hobbies and art forms that crosses boundaries like no other. It has the potential to transform an otherwise lifeless aquarium into a living, evolving slice of nature in your living space that has the potential to enrich your life on so many levels. The entire process—from buying your aquarium and equipment, planning your design, and choosing your hardscape, researching your plants and fish, to watching it develop and grow . . . there's really nothing else like it. Your helping hand guides its progress over the weeks and months and offers rewards that most hobbies cannot provide. An aquascape connects you with nature, gives a sense of serenity and comfort, and allows you to enjoy a different world separated from the stresses and strains of modern life.

As we approach the end of this book my sincere hope is that it has helped to provide you with some of the knowledge and inspiration to give you the best start enabling you to develop your own aquascaping hobby. We have covered all of the necessary topics from choosing your aquarium and necessary equipment, to hardscape and the basics on how to grow healthy plants whilst avoiding algae. The result will hopefully be that you are now confident enough to embark on one of the most exciting, yet relaxing and therapeutic pastimes there are. The techniques and methodologies described here are by no means the only way you can achieve success but they are based on my own experiences; a process of making many mistakes, learning from them and sharing that learning with you. You will probably make your own mistakes too and this is something not to fear. Embrace the lessons that these mistakes provide and as you gain more experience you will become more confident with your ability as an aquascaper, improving all of the time. Continual improvement is better than delayed perfection!

SO WHAT HAPPENS NEXT?

Hopefully you've read, learned from, and enjoyed this book to the point where you can successfully aquascape and be happy with your creation. I think it's a great idea to share your aquascapes with others so they can be inspired and have their lives also improved by the power of aquascaping. If you are comfortable with social media then you could consider sharing your aquascaping journey with the ever-growing online

Me with my friend and colleague, Adam Paszczela (left), in his aquascape gallery in Poland.

community on Facebook, Instagram, YouTube, and the numerous online forums. Most of you reading this will have a smartphone capable of taking great photos and video, and creating content is free. You can engage with other hobbyists and aquascapers, learn from each other, be inspired by one another and help to grow this wonderful hobby beyond the niche space that it currently resides. A few years ago, I was interviewed by a fellow YouTuber and declared that my mission was to see an aquascape in every home. Of course, this is a pipe dream—but we are heading in the right direction. As the human race becomes more reliant on technology and we become increasingly disconnected from nature, let us use this very technology to promote our wonderful hobby and help to serve our fellow humans by sharing the beautiful world of aquascaping.

10 TIPS ON AQUASCAPE SMARTPHONE PHOTOGRAPHY

1. Invest in a tripod with a cellphone mount attachment. They can be bought for a few bucks from a well-known online store.
2. Clean the camera lens with a soft cloth to remove any greasy fingerprints or dirt.
3. Limit any ambient light hitting the aquarium and avoid reflections. Shoot late in evening or early morning and/or draw your curtains/blinds.
4. If possible, place more light on top of the aquarium pointing into the aquascape. The brighter the aquarium lighting, the higher quality the image will be.

5. Compose your image by using the rule of thirds grid on your smartphone camera app. Have your intended focal point line up with the grid lines.
6. Ensure the tripod/camera is dead square to the aquarium. Look closely at the vertical and horizontal lines.
7. Adjust the exposure of the image by touching and holding your finger on the center of the screen, then slide your finger up and down to adjust the exposure. This also locks the autofocus on most smartphones.
8. To avoid any chance of camera shake that can cause motion blur use the timer function on the camera app.
9. Wait patiently for the shot where the fish are in the best position possible.
10. Practice and have fun!

FREQUENTLY ASKED QUESTIONS

I have been answering questions on a wide range of planted aquarium and aquascaping topics since 2006, when I became a regular feature contributor to *Practical Fishkeeping* magazine and part of their "Ask the Expert" panel. Since then, I co-founded the UK Aquatic Plant Society in 2007 (I have over 7,000 posts on their active forum) and given over 100 aquascaping workshops and seminars across the globe. I continue to be active every day on my various social media channels, including Facebook, Instagram, and YouTube. During this time, I have answered literally thousands of questions, with some being asked more than others. Here is my top 10 list of frequently asked questions and my answers that I hope will solidify your understanding of the content in this book.

Q: Why aren't my plants growing?

There are two main factors to consider here. Firstly, ensure your plants are healthy to begin with, i.e., in good condition from the store. Start off with unhealthy plants that have been slowly suffering in a poorly maintained plant holding system and you are unlikely to get a good start with your plants. So make sure to buy your plants as fresh as possible.

Secondly, you need to figure out if your system is appropriate for the plant species you are trying to grow. Consider lighting—do you have enough? Does your chosen species require CO_2 injection? Are you using good quality liquid fertilizers and a nutrient-rich substrate? Is there enough circulation in the aquarium? Are you performing enough water changes? These are all questions you must ask yourself to fully understand the reasoning for any difficulties with plant growth. Chapters Two to Five cover this question in more detail.

Q: How do I get rid of algae?

Algae is very likely a result of poor plant growth in conjunction with a lack of appropriate aquarium maintenance. It is essential to address these issues before looking for a quick fix to treat your current issues, otherwise the algae will continue to return.

To treat algae, first manually remove as much as possible and follow this up with a large water change, as well as giving your filter a good cleaning. Then address the underlying cause of your algae to prevent it from reoccurring. Focus on healthy plant growth—and lots of it—in combination with scrupulous and regular maintenance practice. Chapter Ten covers the topic of algae in more detail.

Q: What plants should I start with?

I always recommend starting out with a large

proportion of easy plants, even if you have a relatively high-energy system capable of growing more demanding plants. Easy plants don't require high levels of light or CO_2 injection and should grow well in the majority of aquariums. (There is a full list of easy plant species at the end of the appendix.) Consider your foreground, midground, background, and epiphyte plants, making sure to choose them according to their size. Your initial planting should include a large quantity of fast-growing species, as these will help prevent algae. Floating plants are also a great idea due to their fast growth and can always be easily removed later once the aquascape has matured. Check out Chapter Eight for more information on choosing plants.

Q: Do I need CO_2 injection?

The simple answer is no, especially if you only intend to grow easy plants. However, if you wish to grow more demanding species it will probably be required. CO_2 injection will improve the growth and overall condition of *all* aquarium plants, so do consider it if you wish to achieve the best results. Those who prefer a more natural approach—especially beginners first getting into the hobby—can begin without CO_2 and then upgrade when ready to do so. Chapter Five looks at CO_2 injection.

Q: Is liquid fertilizer safe for shrimp?

Most liquid fertilizers contain trace amounts of copper that, in large quantities, can be lethal to all invertebrates. However, in all known aquarium-branded liquid fertilizer products, the copper content is very small and completely safe for shrimp—unless you overdose by a huge amount. Copper is, in fact, necessary in tiny amounts for invertebrates, as it is responsible for oxygen transportation in their blood. Find out more information on liquid fertilizers in Chapter Four.

Q: How do I know what aquarium lighting to choose?

A good starting point is to buy an aquarium that comes supplied with lighting and begin with growing easy plants. If and when you wish to grow more difficult species, then consider upgrading your lighting. It can be a confusing process, with so many lighting units now available to retrofit to all sizes of aquariums, so aim for a unit that is a proven performer. You can usually find reviews and read experiences from fellow hobbyists online by performing a simple internet search or by engaging with a reputable community (such as the UK Aquatic Plant Society forum). LED units are the most popular, and as an approximate guide aim for a power rating of 0.5 to 1 watt per gallon of aquarium water. You may require more powerful lighting to grow more demanding species. Chapter Two covers the topic of lighting in much greater detail.

Q: Do I need a special aquarium soil substrate?

No, but you will find your plants grow better with it. Plants can get their required nutrients from their leaves, so you could achieve healthy plant growth in an inert sand or gravel—though the room for error is increased. Soil substrates provide other benefits, such as lowering the aquarium water pH and hardness; their light and porous structure is great for allowing easy root penetration and beneficial bacteria colonization. Shrimp are particularly fond of a soil substrate, as they love to graze the granules for biofilm as a food source. Chapter Four goes into substrates in more detail.

Q: Do fish jump out of open-top aquariums?
It depends on the fish and the aquascape. Some species of fish are more prone to jumping than others; for example, fast swimming, more active fish are more likely to leap than more sedentary species. Densely planted aquascapes with plenty of hiding places and surface cover can help to prevent any jumping. Another tip is having your lighting ramp up and down gradually if possible, as the sudden light or dark can startle fish, causing them to jump.

Q: How do I vacuum the substrate in a densely planted aquarium?
Simply wave your hand just above the substrate and this will lift up any loose waste organic matter into the water column. Then siphon out this waste-laden aquarium water as part of a water change ensuring you remove as much of the floating particles as possible. It also helps to siphon out a bit of water before doing so. This way you'll be able to get more of the waste organic matter. Check out Chapter Ten for more info on maintaining your substrate.

Q: What's the biggest tip you can give anyone who wants to create a successful aquascape?
Read this book cover to cover . . . and practice! Don't be afraid to make mistakes. Learn from them, and you will get better with each attempt. Be patient and don't expect instant results. The journey should be more rewarding than the destination.

And, most importantly: have fun!

ACKNOWLEDGMENTS

Thank you so much to the following friends, brands, and stores for their support in helping to create this book. If you're not listed, and you've been a part of this aquascaping journey, then I'm grateful to you, too.

Adam Paszczela: www.instagram.com/
  adam_paszczela/
Amin Aquatics: www.aminaquatics.co.uk
Annika Reinke: www.garnelenhaus.com
Aquarium Design Group: www.aquariumdesign-
  group.com
Aquarium Gardens: www.aquariumgardens.co.uk
Dennerle: www.dennerle.com
Evolution Aqua: www.evolutionaqua.com
Felix Smart Aquarium: www.felixsmart.com
Fritz Aquatics: www.fritzaquatics.com
Garnelenhaus: www.garnelenhaus.com
Green Aqua: www.greenaqua.hu
Iain Sutherland: www.instagram.com/
  iainsutherland24

Jennifer Williams: www.JWDaqua.com
Jeremy Gay: www.fishkeepingnews.com
Joey Mullen: www.youtube.com/uarujoey
Jurijs Jutjajevs: www.jurijsjutjajevs.com
Michael Mikkelsen: www.instagram.com/
  michaelfmikkelsen
Nathan Hill: www.practicalfishkeeping.co.uk
Oase: www.oase.com
Oliver Knott: www.oliverknott.com
PezVerde: www.pezverde.es
Scaped Nature: www.scapednature.com
Seneye: www.seneye.com
Tannin Aquatics: www.tanninaquatics.com
Tropica Aquarium Plants: www.tropica.com

I have to give special mention to the late, great Takashi Amano who inspired me to start aquascaping. I am sorry we never met. Also a huge thanks to Jason Katzman from Skyhorse Publishing: my tireless editor, fellow hobbyist, and now good friend. And, finally, to my beautiful wife, Emma, whose love, support, and patience knows no limits. Thank you, all.

PHOTOGRAPH CREDITS

All plant photos in Top 40 Popular Plant Species (**Appendix II**) and bulb plant photo (**Chapter Eight**): Tropica Aquarium Plants, www.tropica.com

Golden Ratio and Circles (**Chapter Six**): Fabian Beck (German Aquascaper), www.instagram.com/scapeling

Use of Depth is a Game Changer (**Chapter Six**): PezVerde (Spanish Aquascaping Store), www.pezverde.es

Dutch Style (**Chapter Six**): Joe Harvey (US Aquascaper and online store owner), www.burraqua.com

Diormama Style (**Chapter Six**): Filipe Oliveira and Aquaflora, www.aquaflora.nl

Seneye Reef PAR meter (**Chapter Two**): www.seneye.com

LINKS/SOURCES: ADDITIONAL INFORMATION

RECOMMENDED RESOURCES

UK Aquatic Plant Society: www.ukaps.org/forum

The Barr Report: www.barrreport.com

The Aquatic Gardeners Association: www.aquatic-gardeners.org

The 2hr Aquarist: www.advancedplantedtank.com

The Aquascapers Collective: www.facebook.com/tacscape/

Green Aqua YouTube channel: www.youtube.com/viktorlantos

Flowgrow: https://www.flowgrow.de/db/aquaticplants

Tropica Aquarium Plants: www.tropica.com

Reddit: www.reddit.com/r/aquariums; r/aquascape; r/plantedtank

RECOMMENDED AQUARIUM PRODUCTS

Aqua Design Amano (aquariums and aquascaping products): Annika Reinke: www.garnlenhaus.com www.adana.co.jp/en/

CO_2 Art (CO_2 kit): www.co2art.eu

Dennerle (aquariums, plants and plant care): www.dennerle.com/en/

Felix Smart Aquarium (smart aquarium controller): www.felixsmart.com

Fluval (aquariums): www.fluvalaquatics.com

Fritz Aquatics (water conditioners): www.fritzaquatics.com

Green Leaf Aquarium (CO_2 kit): www.greenleafaquariums.com

Kessil (lighting): www.kessil.com

OASE (aquariums and filters): www.oase.com/en/

The Aquascaper (aquariums and cabinets): www.evolutionaqua.com/aquascaper

Tropica Aquarium Plants (plants and plant care): www.tropica.com

Twinstar (lighting): www.twinstareu.com

Ultum Nature Systems (aquariums): www.ultumnaturesystems.com

RECOMMENDED BOOKS

Amano, Takashi, *Nature Aquarium World, Book 1*; T.F.H. Publications, Inc. (1992)

Amano, Takashi, *Nature Aquarium World, Book 2*; T.F.H. Publications, Inc. (1994)

Amano, Takashi, *Nature Aquarium World, Book 3*; T.F.H. Publications, Inc. (1994)

Amano, Takashi, *Aquarium Plant Paradise*; T.F.H. Publications, Inc. (1999)

Amano, Takashi, *Nature Aquarium: Complete Works 1985–2009*; T.F.H. Publications, Inc. (2011)

Amano, Takashi, *Origin of Creation*; Aqua Design Amano Co.,Ltd. (2016)

Kasselmann, Christel, *Planted Aquariums: Creation and Maintenance*; Krieger Publishing Company (2005)

Kasselmann, Christel, *Aquarium Plants*; Christel Kasselmann / Aquarium Plants Publisher (2020)

Randall, Karen A., *Sunken Gardens*: *A Step-by-Step Guide to Planting Freshwater Aquariums*; Timber Press (2017)

Sweeney, Mary E., *101 Best Aquarium Plants: How to Choose Hardy, Vibrant, Eye-Catching Species That Will Thrive in Your Home Aquarium*; T.F.H. Publications, Inc. (2008)

ABOUT THE AUTHOR

George Farmer is an internationally renowned aquascaper and planted aquarium expert from the UK, where he lives with his wife, Emma, two stepsons and daughter, Harrison, Toby, and Florence, and miniature schnauzer, Tommy. He has hundreds of articles and photographs published in magazines from the UK, USA, Germany, and France, and has been a guest on primetime TV, radio, and podcasts. George has aquascaped for the Royal Horticultural Society and has traveled all over the world to give aquascaping workshops and keynote addresses. He co-founded the UK Aquatic Plant Society in 2007, and has a large following on his YouTube and Instagram channels where his aquascaping videos have had over 25 million views at the time of writing. George's other hobbies include keeping fit, biohacking, and gaming.

YouTube: www.youtube.com/gf225
Instagram: www.instagram.com/georgefarmerstudios

APPENDICES

APPENDIX I: STEP-BY-STEP AQUASCAPES

AQUASCAPER 300 CUBE

1. This is an Aquascaper 300 Cube aquarium that measures 12 x 12 x 12 in (30 x 30 x 30 cm) that has a total volume of 7.1 gal (27 L). It doesn't come supplied with a light, filter or heater so these need to be chosen and fitted appropriately. I like to use external filters and heaters wherever possible as they don't take up valuable physical and visual space inside the aquarium. It's an open-top rimless tank so a form of suspended lighting or clip-on lighting is required. Here I am using a Cherry iNano LED lamp that provides 20 watts and

is dimmable. A small quantity of cosmetic sand is added to the foreground with the rear of the aquarium remaining empty, ready for aquarium soil. The sand is inert and not designed for rooted plants but adds a natural look to the foreground. Open sand foregrounds are popular for aquascapes where carpeting plants are not desired. They still look great but are much lower maintenance than their live plant counterparts.

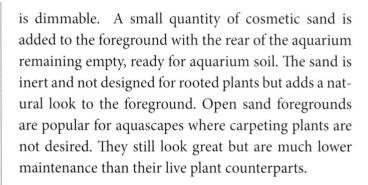

2. Rocks are positioned on top of sand with half of the rocks overlapping the bare bottom of the aquarium. The idea is that the rocks look great but also

provide a physical barrier between the aquarium soil and sand. These rocks are known as Grey Mountain rock, but these particular types have a yellow hue. This matched perfectly with the color of the sand in front. It is important to consider how the rocks and any cosmetic sand or gravel (without plants) harmonize or contrast to give the best overall impact. This is a great example of harmonizing, but you could also deliberately opt for a contrasting effect; for example, using a white sand and black lava stone. It is usually advisable to avoid the use of very fine sand as this will show up any dirt and debris immediately. It is also liable to compact over time and cause areas of excess anaerobic bacteria.

3. Aquarium soil is added to the background behind the rocks. This is ideal for planting into and provides a host of benefits including feeding the plants with nutrients and lowering the aquarium water pH and hardness. It doesn't need to be pre-washed and planting into it is very simple using aquascaping tweezers. Some soils can leech ammonia so it's important to ensure the water is safe before adding livestock by testing for ammonia and nitrite. Most soils will supply nutrients for at least 12 months and can last for several years, especially if the plants are well-fed using a comprehensive liquid fertilizer and root capsules. The soil is prevented from migrating onto the sand foreground by the barrier of rocks. Any gaps between the rocks can be blocked with filter floss or smaller stones.

4. One beautiful piece of Redmoor Root is added. This type of wood is known to float when first added to an aquarium so I have pre-soaked it for several weeks prior. If you do not have time for this you can weigh it down with rocks or even use a non-toxic glue to attach it to the rocks. Another option is to glue it to the aquarium base before adding the substrate. I love this wood because it offers loads of opportunities to add epiphyte plants by simply pushing the roots and rhizomes into the spaces between the branches. Some new woods can get covered in a bacterial or fungal growth that looks a milky white color after the first few days. This is

harmless but can be easily removed with a toothbrush and siphoned it away during a water change.

5. Now the plants are added into the soil. I use aquascaping tweezers to plant two species of crypt: *Cryptocoryne undulatus* "Red" and *Cryptocoryne willisii*. These act as a midground transition between the rocks and the background stem plants. Transitions between the foreground and background are important to give the aquascape an overall sense of depth. If you went immediately from a low foreground plant to a tall background plant the contrast in height would look excessive and unnatural. Mastering the use of the

midground in aquascaping is a key component to success, whether it's from using effective hardscape design or planting layout.

6. The background stem plant, *Pogostemon erectus*, is added to the rear of the aquarium using aquascaping tweezers. Tweezers are essential here because to use your fingers would prove very challenging in such a confined space. In total around 10 stems are added all across the back. The more plants you have the better the start-up phase because these plants help to prevent nuisance algae. *Pogostemon erectus* is a medium-paced grower and, ideally, I would mix this with some fast

growing weeds such as *Hygrophila* "Siamensis 53B" or *Limnophila sessiflora*. Unfortunately, at the time of aquascaping, this was all I had access to!

7. The final plants to be added are the epiphyte plants. These are species that need to be attached to the hard-scape rather than being planted into the substrate/soil. I attach a combination of *Microsorum pteropus* "Trident," *Anubias* "Petite," and *Bucephalandra sp*. To attach the plants, I simply wedge them in-between the rocks and wood. For other spaces, I use a gel-type cyanoacrylate superglue. It's important to use as little glue

as possible to prevent any unsightly white portions of glue showing. Also be mindful not to glue your fingers together—trust me, I have done this many times! Over time the rhizomes (the portion of the plant where the leaves grow from) self-attach to the hardscape keeping them secure.

8. Now I add the water slowly using a kitchen colander. I pump the water in slowly from my kitchen using a submergible pump and bucket at a temperature of around 72°F/24°C with a dechlorinator. Fun fact: I've had this red colander since I started keeping aquariums

9. After 3 months the aquascape is approaching full maturity and provides a great home for my cherry shrimp. After a few weeks I added some mosses and *Riccardia chamedryfolia* between the rocks. Adding this later is a good idea to help prevent them getting covered in any potential algae that is common in new set-ups. Weekly maintenance is carried out by performing water changes and cleaning the aquarium glass and filter in old aquarium water. CO_2 injection is added via the Tropica CO_2 Nano System that helps to provide lush plant growth in conjunction with Tropica Specialised Nutrition at 1 ml per day. The shrimp breed well in this aquascape, which is very rewarding to experience. Excess shrimp are given away to hobbyist friends or added to my other larger aquariums!

almost twenty years ago and I even have a t-shirt featuring it! I use it to fill all of my aquariums. The colander disperses the water so it doesn't disturb the soil which would otherwise cause clouding and uproot the plants. Once the tank is filled the filter and heater are switched on and the light is plugged into a timer and set for 8 hours per day. I change 50 percent of the water every day for the first week, then 50 percent every other day for week 2 and 50 percent every third day for week 3. After 4 weeks I change 50 percent every week. Liquid fertilizer is added daily after 2 weeks at 2 ml per day using Tropica Premium Nutrition.

Aquarium Specifications

Aquarium	Evolution Aqua Aquascaper 300 Cube
Lighting	Cherry Aqua iNano LED (20 watts, dimmable) for 8 hours per day
Filtration	OASE FiltoSmart 100 Thermo with glass inlet and outlet
CO_2	Tropica CO_2 System Nano with Aquario NEO CO_2 diffuser
Substrate	Tropica Aquarium Soil Power (1 x 3 L bags)
Liquid Fertilizers	Tropica Specialised Nutrition (1 ml per day)
Hardscape	Redmoor Root, Grey Mountain Rock
Plants	*Microsorum pteropus* "Trident," *Anubias* "Petite" and "Pangolino," Various *Bucephalandra* species, *Cryptocroyne undulatus* "Red," *Cryptocoryne willisii*, *Pogostemon erectus*, *Riccardia chamedryfolia*, *Taxiphyllum* "Spikey"
Shrimp	Cherry shrimp (*Neocaridina davidii*)

AQUASCAPER 1200

1. We are using an Aquascaper 1200 rimless aquarium measuring 48 x 18 x 24 in (120 x 45 x 60 cm) with a total volume of 85 gal (324 L). The glass is low iron, giving it a higher clarity than regular float glass. The silicone

is clear that adds to the invisible effect of the aquarium that we are trying to achieve. There is no background and the pale wall behind is illuminated from the over-tank lighting that provides a greater sense of depth and more natural feel.

2. Next we add our substrate. In this case it's Tropica Aquarium Soil, a proven performer that I have used in

over fifty aquascapes. It's nutrient content and structure make it ideal for plant growth and it doesn't require any pre-rinsing or additional products. Four 9-L bags are used in total. It is not the cheapest substrate available, but it is wise to invest in a good quality soil to help achieve the best results.

3. The hardscape process comes next and it's worth reminding you that this is an essential part of the whole aquascape. Start off with a strong hardscape composition and it becomes far easier to create a successful aquascape. Here I have used a large piece of Frodo Stone; a beautiful rock type that originates from eastern Europe. I am very lucky to be friends with one of Europe's largest dealers of Frodo Stone, Adam Paszczela, who sent me over these wonderful pieces. The largest piece is placed in accordance with the rule of thirds in order to provide aesthetic balance.

4. The next size down rock is added next. Care is taken to ensure the rocks compliment each other and look natural. You should spend as much time as you need during this process. It is helpful to analyze each rock by looking at each side on all axes to determine how and where it should be positioned in the layout. It is often case of trial and error, taking a step back to reflect on your choice before making any adjustments. Repeat this process until you are 100 percent content with your final decision.

5. Driftwood is added next. This large piece has been pre-soaked so I will know it will sink once the aquarium is filled with water. This soaking process also helps to reduce any potential tannin staining that many occur. Many wood types will can leech these tea-like compounds that discolor the aquarium water. If this does occur, then frequent water changes and/or chemical filtration with activated carbon can prove helpful. As with the rocks, it is best to start with the largest

piece of wood and ensure it is positioned in a natural and aesthetically balanced manner.

6. The remaining rocks and wood are added. I have done this under water to prevent the wood from drying out. I usually recommend the entire hardscape process is done in a dry aquarium if possible to make it less

messy, but in this case I was keen not to allow the wood to dry out. The pieces of wood and rocks are positioned carefully again to ensure a pleasant and natural effect. This part of aquascaping is really down to your own creativity so have fun with it and take your time. Don't be afraid to try something a little crazy! You can always make adjustments further down the line.

7. Now it's time to start planting. I usually begin with the foreground plants and here I'm using *Cryptocoryne parva*. This is a slow growing and easy plant ideal for all sizes of aquarium. I split each pot into several portions and plant them using aquascaping tweezers. Using fingers becomes very challenging especially with smaller plants. Your fingers will excessively disturb the soil surrounding the plant, which often leads to the plant floating away from the soil. Tweezers are an essential tool for any aquascaper!

8. Moving onto the midground and background plants I'm using more *Cryptocoryne*. I love these plants

because they are slow growing, meaning less maintenance with virtually no trimming necessary for months. They require less light than many plants and can also grow well without CO_2 injection, making them ideal for budget-friendly systems. They do best with a

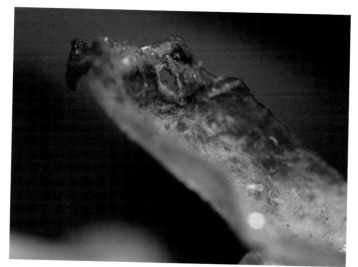

An example of what "Crypt melt" can look like.

nutrient-rich substrate and good quality liquid fertilizer. Interestingly, they often change color, shape and size depending on the conditions they are kept. Some crypts can struggle when adapting to their new home and shed their leaves—a condition commonly known as crypt melt. Good news is that new leaves will grow back readily adapted to their new conditions.

9. The final plants are added by attaching them to the wood and rocks. These are epiphyte plants that need to have their rhizomes (part of plant where the leaves grow from) exposed to circulating water. They are attached by wedging them in-between gaps in the wood and rocks, or by supergluing them with a gel-type cyanoacrylate glue. Cotton thread or fishing line can also be used to attach them. Epiphyte plants are great because they add an immediate sense of maturity to the aquascape. They are mostly easy plants too that are slow growing which make them suitable for

low-maintenance and lower energy setups. I am using a combination of *Microsorum pteropus* "Trident" and *Anubias* "Petite," with some portions of *Taxiphyllum* "Spikey" moss glued to the wood and rocks.

10. Two weeks after planting, some plant growth is evident and I've added some floating plants to help deal with some minor algae issues. Floating plants are great because they shade the lower plants, take up excess nutrients and produce extra oxygen through their roots. Because they are nearer the light and have unlimited access to CO_2 in the air they grow very quickly. This helps to deal with algae and any pale growth indicates a lack of nutrients making them a perfect "indicator" plant. During the first few weeks it is essential to change plenty (at least 50 percent) of the aquarium water frequently (at least three times per week) to also help prevent algae. Lighting is set using a timer for 6 to 8 hours and the CO_2 injection is set to the appropriate dosing rate. Liquid fertilizers are added after two weeks every day.

11. Two months after planting and you can see considerable growth. I have swapped the very slow growing *Crpytocoryne parva* for *Helanthium tenellum* "Green," which is much faster growing, giving a more lush and fresh appearance. The faster growth also results in less risk of algae. I have also added some *Hygrophila* "Siamensis 53B" to the background, which is another fast grower giving a dense bushy feel. The lesson for me here was that I needed to use a lot more fast-growing plants to help deal with the algae issues that were occurring. You can just see the recently added red stem plant, *Limnophila hippuroides* that I added because I wanted more color. Over the coming weeks this

beautiful and relatively easy plant this will become a dominant component to the aquascape.

12. Here is the aquascape after four months of growth. I have added more plants including the red stem plant in the background, *Limnophila hippuroides.* You can see I have also rearranged the wood slightly. Making adjustments like this is a great idea to evolve the aquascape over time in a way that will give you the best overall impression to suit your taste. Aquascaping with live plants is a unique art form because as the plants grow, they can change the whole balance of the aquarium and we can use this to our advantage. You can see how the crypts have developed beautifully and the epiphyte plants have matured to give a lush and complete look to the aquascape.

Aquarium Specifications

Aquarium	Evolution Aqua Aquascaper 1200
Lighting	Twinstar 1200SA
Filtration	Oase Biomaster 600 Thermo
CO$_2$	Pressurised refillable system with GLA regulator and CO$_2$ Art inline diffuser
Substrate	Tropica Aquarium Soil (4 x 9 L bags)
Liquid Fertilizers	Tropica Specialised Nutrition (20 ml per day)
Hardscape	Driftwood and Frodo Stone
Plants	*Helanthium tenellum* "Green," *Cryptocoryne parva, Cryptocoryne willisii, Cryptocoryne undulatus* "Red," *Cryptocoryne wendtii* "Green," *Cryptocoryne wendtii* "Tropica," *Cryptocoryne beckettii* "Petchii," *Limnophila hippuroides, Hygrophila* "Siamensis 53B," *Microsorum pteropus* "Trident," *Anubias* "Petite," *Taxiphyllum* "Spikey"
Fish	Pearl gourami (*Trichopodus leerii*), Harlequin rasbora (*Trigonostigma heteramorpha*)
Invertebrates	Amano shrimp (*Caridina multidentata*), Cherry shrimp (*Neocaridina davidii*), Nerite snail (*Neritina natalensis*)

DENNERLE NANOCUBE

1. This Dennerle NanoCube aquarium has a total volume of 15.7 gal (60 L) and is quite unique with it being slightly taller than it is long and wide. This becomes an important consideration when aquascaping to ensure the height is best used for visual impact. It's a rimless tank that comes with a kit supplied with an internal corner filter and 8-watt LED light unit. There is also the option to buy this tank on its own so you can choose your own filtration and lighting solutions, which may be required for more advanced aquascapes with more demanding plant species. The rounded front corners are an attractive feature allowing for a unique viewing experience when viewed from the sides.

2. A layer of cosmetic gravel is added to the foreground, leaving the rear part of the aquarium bare and ready for aquarium soil to be added later. This attractive gravel has a red/orange hue and its grain size is large enough to not allow for compaction over time. Because there will be no plants added to the gravel there is no need to add a nutrient-rich base layer or root capsules, although hardy foreground plants could be used later if desired. The open foreground look is popular for

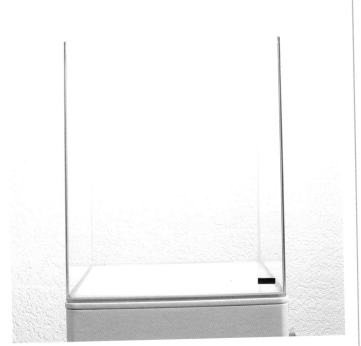

aquascapers who don't want the hassle of growing a carpeting plant that generally requires higher levels of lighting, nutrients and circulation.

3. A selection of red sandstone rocks are added between the gravel and the bare base of the aquarium. These rocks harmonize beautifully with the color and texture of the foreground gravel. The biggest rock is positioned in accordance with the rule of thirds compositional guideline. Being the most dominant feature in the foreground, it provides a focal area making it essential to place it with care and attention. The

remaining smaller rocks are added to the sides in a manner to look as attractive as possible. This rock type does not influence the water chemistry although it is a great idea to thoroughly wash your hardscape before aquascaping.

4. Aquarium soil is added to the background behind the rocks. This is ideal for planting into and provides a host of benefits including feeding the plants with nutrients and lowering the aquarium water pH and hardness. It doesn't need to be pre-washed and planting into it is very simple using aquascaping tweezers.

Most soils have a high cation exchange capacity (CEC), meaning they can uptake nutrients from the aquarium water and make those nutrients available to the plant roots. The soil is prevented from migrating onto the sand foreground by the barrier of rocks. Any gaps between the rocks can be blocked with filter floss or smaller stones.

5. Probably the most important stage in this aquascape is the selection and positioning of the main wood pieces, as these are the dominant feature. Four pieces of driftwood are chosen to suit the size and shape of this aquarium, making best use of the height. The wood is

arranged in a way to look as natural and well-balanced as possible, whilst providing some areas to attach epiphyte plants and moss. This type of wood may float so it's important to secure it appropriately. Here I have simply wedged it between the stones and under the soil. Care must be taken during the filling process to monitor any movement of the wood. I have learned the hard way and have unfortunately experienced the devastation that floating wood can cause on a new aquascape—tearing up the plants and clouding the water!

6. Tall background plants are added to the background. This is *Eleocharis vivipara* that added a wonderful fine

textured backdrop. Just in front of the *Eleocharis* I plant some *Blyxa japonica* that has a similar vertical texture, providing harmony. In the foreground some moss-covered lava stones are around the rocks and wood to add extra interest. These also add a sense of maturity to the aquascape right away. Eventually the moss will creep over the adjacent pieces of wood and rock, helping to create an ancient forest feel to the aquascape.

7. The final plants to be added are the epiphyte plants. These are species that need to be attached to the hardscape rather than being planted into the substrate/

soil. I attach a combination of *Taxiphyllum barberei*, *Hygrophila pinnatifida*, and *Bucephalandra* "Brownie." To attach the plants, I simply wedge them in-between the rocks and wood. For the mosses I use a gel-type cyanoacrylate superglue. Gel-type glue is better than the regular liquid especially when gluing on vertical surfaces to prevent the glue from running. Any glue that's not completely covered by the plants will show up with its white color so it's important to use as little as possible.

8. Twigs are added around the main pieces of driftwood to add extra texture and a sense of interest and

natural feel. These details really add a whole dynamic to the aquascape that would otherwise look relatively plain. It is worth experimenting yourselves by mixing differing materials together and see how they turn out. If it doesn't look great, then simply remove them. By practicing over and over you will improve each time. Don't be afraid to make mistakes—they are the best way to learn!

9. Now I add the water slowly using an external filter inlet tube and strainer. I pump the water in slowly at a temperature of around 72°F/24°C with a dechlorinator.

The strainer disperses the water so it doesn't disturb the soil which would otherwise cause clouding and uproot the plants.

10. Once the tank is filled the filter and heater are switched on and the light is plugged into a timer and set for 8 hours per day. I change 50 percent of the water every day for the first week, then 50 percent every other day for week 2 and 50 percent every third day for week 3. After 4 weeks I change 50 percent every week. Liquid fertilizer is added daily after 2 weeks at 2 ml per day using Dennerle Scaper's Green.

Aquarium Specifications

Aquarium	Dennerle NanoCube 60
Lighting	Dennerle 8w LED
Filtration	Dennerle Corner Filter XL
CO_2	None added
Substrate	Dennerle Scapers Soil (1 x 8 L bag) and natural gravel
Liquid Fertilizers	Dennerle Scaper's Green, 2 ml per day
Hardscape	Red sandstone, Driftwood, twigs
Plants	*Eleocharis vivipara, Blyxa japonica, Bucephalandra* "Brownie," *Hygrophila pinnatifida, Taxiphyllum barberei*

DENNERLE SCAPERS TANK

1. This Dennerle Scapers Tank has a total volume of 14.5 gal (55 L). It is ideal for aquascaping because its front-to-rear depth is larger than its height. As such, this bigger footprint provides more space for creating a sense depth in the aquascape. It has attractive rounded corners at the front and, being a rimless aquarium, allows for hardscape and plants to protrude from the surface (if desired). It can be purchased as a tank-only product, giving you options to fit your own choice of filtration and lighting, or as a complete system with supplied filter and lighting.

2. Three pieces of Mopani wood are added. They are positioned in a manner to give a natural aesthetic balance, and the pieces are intertwined to give the illusion that it is one larger piece of wood. This wood has been pre-soaked for many months, meaning it does not leech any tannins that will otherwise discolor the water. New Mopani wood is well known to stain the water, which can be beneficial if you wish to create a blackwater-style

aquascape. For clear water, large frequent water changes—in conjunction with chemical filtration, such as activated carbon or Seachem Purigen—will be necessary. Care also needs to be taken to ensure the wood doesn't float after filling. Rocks can be placed on top or it can be glued to the aquarium glass bottom using an aquarium-safe glue, such as JBL Haru.

3. A selection of red sandstone rocks are added between the gravel and the bare base of the aquarium. These rocks harmonize beautifully with the color and texture of the foreground gravel. The biggest rock is positioned in accordance with the rule of thirds compositional guideline. Being the most dominant feature in the foreground, it provides a focal area making it essential to place it with care and attention. The remaining smaller rocks are added to the sides in a manner to look as attractive as possible.

This rock type does not influence the water chemistry, although it is best to thoroughly wash your rocks before aquascaping.

4. Aquarium soil is added to the rear of the aquarium, leaving some open space in the foreground for the cosmetic gravel. The soil is sloped toward the back, which gives the optical illusion that the aquascape is deeper (front to back) than it really is. The soil provides numerous benefits to the entire aquarium system, including better plant root growth and pH and hardness lowering of the water that most fish, shrimp, and plants prefer. It is more expensive than regular gravel or sand but is a worthwhile investment if you want the best from your aquarium plants. Some soils can produce ammonia in the initial two weeks or so, so it's important to dilute this with large and frequent water changes.

5. Rocks are added just in front of the soil. Seven pieces of Seiryu Stone are used that look great with their interesting textures, which also create a physical barrier to help stop the soil from migrating onto the gravel foreground that will be added next. Seiryu Stone is a limestone-based rock that can increase the pH and hardness of your aquarium water. However, this should not be an issue with regular water changes that help to keep the water parameters relatively stable. Over time, the rocks can form an algae coating that can be manually removed with a toothbrush or by using appropriate algae eaters such as Nerite snails.

6. Gravel is added to the foreground in front of the rocks. This is called Baikal gravel from Dennerle and requires a thorough rinsing beforehand to prevent it from clouding the aquarium water. The color and textures of the gravel harmonize well with the stones.

It's important to always consider how a foreground cosmetic gravel or sand contrasts or blends with the hardscape behind it so you can achieve the best overall impression. Baikal gravel does have sharp edges so it is important not to stock fish with sensitive barbels such as loach species.

7. Background plants are inserted into the soil using aquascaping tweezers. We are using a mixture of crypts that remain small: *Cryptocoryne parva* and *Cryptocoryne lutea* "Hobbit." The hairgrass species *Eleocharis acicularis* is planted in between the crypts, which adds a natural blend of textures. Over the longer term, the hairgrass will gradually form a full carpet spreading around the crypts. It's important to prevent an excess build-up of waste organics among these plants. I like to wave my hand just above the plants

their rhizomes exposed to circulating water. If they are buried in the substrate, the rhizome can suffocate and kill the plant. Here we are using a several varieties of *Anubias*, *Bucephalandra*, and mosses. They are all slow growing and easy plants suitable for most aquariums, with or without CO_2 injection. I particularly enjoy adding epiphyte plants right at the end of the planting process, as it really helps to bring the aquascape to life and adds an immediate sense of maturity.

during a water change and siphon out the lifted detritus during the aquarium water removal.

8. All of the epiphyte plants are added. These are plants that do best attached to the hardscape and need

9. Once the tank is filled, I fit the aquarium filter and lighting. I change 50 percent of the water every day for the first week, then 50 percent every other day for week 2 and 50 percent every third day for week 3. After 4 weeks, I change 50 percent every week. Liquid fertilizer is added daily after 2 weeks at 2 ml per day using Dennerle Scaper's Green.

Aquarium Specifications

Aquarium	Dennerle Scapers Tank
Lighting	Dennerle Trocal LED 40 18w
Filtration	Dennerle Scapers Flow
CO_2	None added
Substrate	Dennerle Scapers Soil (1 x 4 L bag) and Baikal Natural Gravel
Liquid Fertilizers	Dennerle Scaper's Green, 2 ml per day
Hardscape	Mopani Wood, Seiryu Stone
Plants	*Eleocharis acicularis, Crytocoryne lutea* "Hobbit," *Crytocoryne parva, Anubias, Bucephalandra,* mosses

FLUVAL FLEX

1. I am using a Fluval Flex aquarium that hold 15 gal (57 L). This is a great beginner-friendly aquarium because it comes supplied with an LED light capable of growing easy plants and a good quality filtration system built into the background. There is also a space for a heater if you wish to keep tropical fish, although no heater is supplied with the kit. The vertical bow front gives the aquarium a unique style and the black finish contrasts well with the plants and fish. All-in-one kits like this are an ideal introduction to the aquascaping hobby because they take a lot of guesswork out of having to choose the right equipment to build your own system.

2. The substrate is added to the base of the aquarium. In this case I am using Tropica Aquarium Soil (2 x 3 L bags) as this is a proven performer and helps to supply nutrients to the plant roots. It also slightly softens the aquarium water and reduces the pH, making it ideal for most plants and fish. Two pieces of driftwood are

added towards the center of the aquarium. The wood is selected and positioned carefully to give a pleasing and natural visual impact with good height. The wood is pre-soaked to ensure it doesn't float after the aquarium is filled with water. The structure of the wood means that attaching epiphyte plants will be straightforward.

3. Three rocks are added around the base of the wood. They are positioned to give a natural balance and care is given to avoid symmetry. The rocks are also partially buried in the soil which helps to enhance the overall natural appearance. I am using Frodo Stone that has a light grey color contrasting well against the dark soil and black background. I have deliberately chosen relatively small rocks to ensure there remains sufficient space to plant into the soil. It's important to plant densely to help get the best start possible. It helps

to avoid algae issues and also provides a great visual impact right from day one.

4. The foreground is planted using *Helanthium tenellum* "Green" from the Tropica 1-2-Grow range. This is a tissue cultured plants grown in laboratory conditions resulting in a plant that's guaranteed to be free from algae, pest snails, pesticides and disease. The plants are very small because they are young but there is a much higher quantity when compared with regular potted plants. They're also grown in a nutrient dense liquid media that means they are already adapted to growing under water. This results in the plant immediately being able to grow well in the aquarium right after planting. *Helanthium tenellum* "Green" is an easy carpeting plant that will eventually form a solid lawn after several weeks, even without CO_2 injection or high lighting levels.

5. Next I plant the midground with *Cryptocoryne wendtii* "Tropica." This is a beautiful crypt that does well in most setups because it's adaptable to a wide range of water chemistries, it doesn't need CO_2 injection or high light and it's also a slow grower, meaning less maintenance. I love crypts, especially as a midground plant. They often gradually change color and leaf shape over the weeks and months as they mature with different species responding differently depending on your individual setup. Some crypts can shed their leaves soon after planting but do not worry. This crypt "melt" is the plant adapting and new leaves will soon grow back.

6. Background plants are added next. *Hygrophila* "Siamensis 53B" provides a great backdrop with its bright green foliage and interesting textures. This super easy stem plant will grow in almost any setup and because it's a relatively fast grower it is great at helping

to prevent algae. It can be trimmed back when required and this will promote new bushy growth because from wherever you trim the stem two new shoots will emerge. You can re-plant the cutting to create a higher plant density. Over time the plant may become top-heavy with the lower portions becoming starved of light. In this case you can remove the entire plant, trim off the healthiest growing tips and re-plant those.

7. The final plants to be added are the epiphyte plants. These are species that need to be attached to the hardscape rather than being planted into the substrate/soil. I attach a combination of *Microsorum pteropus* and *Anubias* "Petite." To attach the plants, I simply wedge them in-between the rocks and wood. Over time the rhizomes (the portion of the plant where the leaves grow from) self-attached to the hardscape, keeping

them secure. You can also use a cyanoacrylate-based superglue or cotton thread/fishing line to attach the plants but I like to keep it simple, if possible, by simply wedging them in place.

8. Now I add the water slowly using a kitchen colander. I pump the water in slowly from my kitchen using a submergible pump and bucket at a temperature of around 72°F/24°C with a dechlorinator. I use it to fill all of my aquariums. The colander disperses the water so it doesn't disturb the soil which would otherwise cause clouding and uproot the plants. Once the tank is filled the filter and heater are switched on and the light is plugged into a timer and set for 8 hours per day. I change 50 percent of the water every day for the first week, then 50 percent every other day for week 2 and 50 percent every third day for week 3. After 4 weeks, I change 50 percent every week. Liquid fertilizer is added daily after 2 weeks at 2 ml per day using Tropica Premium Nutrition.

9. After 2 months the aquascape is approaching full maturity and provides a great home for my male betta fish. Weekly maintenance is carried out by performing water changes, cleaning the aquarium glass and filter sponge in old aquarium water. I love this aquascape because it shows that you can achieve a beautiful aquascape with a relatively low budget and low maintenance making it achievable by the vast majority of hobbyists, no matter their experience.

Aquarium Specifications

Aquarium	Fluval Flex 15 gal (57 L)
Lighting	Built-in LED approx. 11 watts
Filtration	Built-in background chamber with sponge, carbon and bio-media, 300 lph pump
CO_2	None added
Substrate	Tropica Aquarium Soil (2 x 3 L bags)
Liquid Fertilizers	Tropica Premium Nutrition (1 pump / 2 ml per day)
Hardscape	Two pieces of Sumatra Wood
Plants	*Helanthium tenellum* "Green," *Cryptocoryne wendtii* "Tropica," *Hygrophila* "Siamensis 53B," *Microsorum pteropus*, *Anubias* "Petite"
Fish	Siamese fighting fish (*Betta splendens*)

APPENDIX II: TOP 40 POPULAR PLANT SPECIES

Choosing what plants to use in your aquascape is an exciting yet potentially daunting process with so many available species to choose from. It's important to know if your aquarium system is going to be capable of growing your chosen plants as well as understanding where best to position them in the aquascape.

Here are 40 popular aquarium plant species that are widely available in most countries. They have been split into categories where they are best positioned in the aquascape, i.e., foreground, midground, background, epiphytes and moss (attached to hardscape), floating plants and bulbs. The color code also indicates how demanding each species is in terms of its lighting and nutrient requirements so you can choose your plants according to where they are best suited in your aquarium and if they are likely to thrive. A full species list can be found in the appendix.

Color codes explained

Green—Easy and beginner-friendly plants that should grow well with lower levels of lighting without CO_2 injection. A nutrient-rich substrate and regular liquid fertilizer dosing will give the best results, but they are not always necessary.

Brown—Medium demand category plants will require higher levels of lighting and CO_2 injection to thrive. A high-quality substrate and regular fertilizer dosing will also be necessary.

Red—Advanced category plants will need high levels of lighting and CO_2 injection, as well as frequent liquid fertilizer dosing and a nutrient-rich substrate.

FOREGROUND

Helanthium tenellum "Green"

Previously named *Echinodorus tenellus*, this is a fast growing, easy and undemanding foreground carpeting plant that send out runners to eventually form a full carpet. Leaves usually reach 2–4 in (5–10 cm) tall. Unlike many plants it grows taller with more light and lower lighting keeps it compact.

Marsilea hirsuta

Marsilea hirsuta is a relatively slow growing carpeting plant that will tolerate low lighting, but to promote a tight carpet effect CO_2 injection and moderate lighting may be required. Its leaves form an attractive round shape at up to 1/2 in (1 cm) that are a relatively dark green compared with many other plants, providing a good contrast.

and given enough time will reward you with a full carpet. It's an ideal plant to use in the foreground for low-maintenance aquascapes.

Staurogyne repens

Staurogyne repens is a popular and relatively plant new to the hobby. It's an easy foreground to midground plant that I often like to use as a transitional plant between foreground carpeting plants and hardscape. It's an easy plant but will benefit from a nutrient-rich substrate with its large root structure. Trimming the stems results in new side shoots that encourage a dense bushy appearance.

Cryptocoryne parva

Cryptocoryne parva is one of the smallest species of the popular *Cryptocoryne* family rarely reaching over 1.5 in (4 cm) tall. It's a very slow grower that will definitely benefit from stronger light, CO_2 injection and a nutrient-rich substrate. It eventually sends out runners

Eleocharis acicularis "Mini"

This dwarf hairgrass species is a very popular carpeting plant with needle-like blades. It sends out runners and given enough light and CO_2 will soon form a solid carpet that resembles a well-manicured lawn. It's a good idea to split the plant into as many portions as possible during the planting process to achieve the most economical coverage.

Micranthemum "Monte Carlo"

Commonly known simply as "Monte Carlo," this is a relatively new plant to the hobby but is already one of the most popular carpeting species. With its small bright green round leaves and ability to carpet even in a non-CO_2 injected aquarium with moderate lighting it's a firm favorite with many aquascapers. In the right conditions it can even be used as an epiphyte plant by simply wedging portions amongst hardscape.

Pogostemon helferi

This beautiful foreground plant is characterized by its unique leaves with their crinkled surface and star-like growth pattern, giving it its nickname, "Downoi," that translates to "Little star." The stems can be trimmed to promote side shoots and attractive bushes can be formed. In small aquariums it can be used as a midground plant. Good nutrition is essential to prevent pale growth.

Hemianthus callitrichoides "Cuba"

This very popular carpeting plant was discovered in Cuba by Tropica's founder, Holger Windeløv, and became commonly available in the hobby from 2005. It can be quite demanding of light and CO_2 and will benefit greatly from a soil substrate. Planting can be a challenge due to its delicate root structure but once established can form a beautiful dense carpet with its tiny round leaves.

Glossostigma elatinoides

Simply known as "Glosso" among hobbyists, this classic carpeting plant was made famous by Takashi Amano in his earlier aquascapes from the early to mid-1990s.

It's a relatively demanding plant requiring strong light and good CO_2 and circulation to get the best growth. Too little light will often result in the plant growing upwards instead of sending out horizontal runner. A very fast grower that requires regular trimming once established.

MIDGROUND

Cryptocoryne wendtii "Green"

This is one of the easiest and most adaptable plants capable of thriving in very low light without CO_2 injection.

Cryptocoryne x willisii

As with all *Cryptocoryne* species it has a strong root structure so will benefit from a nutrient-rich substrate or root-feeding capsules. Stronger light can induce interesting colors forming on the leaves such as a reddish hue on the leaf underside.

Cryptocoryne wendtii "Tropica"
Arguably one of the most interesting crypts with its dark green to dark brown leaf color and crinkled leaves. Its growth pattern is interesting with its leaves spreading out quite flat if given sufficient space. Good lighting, nutrients and CO_2 injection will reward you with beautiful shiny leaves. Its unique color and texture make it ideal to use in contrast with greener plants.

This bright green and narrow leaf crypt is perfect for adding to the midground behind a carpeting plant. It's a slow grower that will occasionally send out runners, making it suitable for low-maintenance aquascapes. It will tolerate low light and CO_2 injection isn't necessary but a nutrient-rich substrate is recommended.

Sagittaria subulata

Sagittaria subulata is an easy and very fast-growing plant that sends out runners prolifically. Its eventual height depends on the growing conditions and can vary from a few inches to reaching the entire height of your aquarium. In most situations it will require thinning out regularly to prevent it from taking over the entire aquascape.

Hygrophila pinnatifida

This interesting plant was introduced to the hobby in 2010 and quickly became very popular with its uniquely shaped and serrated leaves. Under stronger light the leaves turn a reddish color and growth becomes more compact. A common aquascaping technique is to use it as an epiphyte plant by attached to wood or rocks. Once established, it's a fast grower that needs regular trimming.

Hydrocotyle tripartita

Originally known as *Hydrocotyle sp.* "Japan," this fast-growing plant readily sends out runners and can quickly smother an aquascape if given the opportunity. It can be planted into the substrate as a carpeting plant or attached as an epiphyte plant. I have grown it without CO_2 injection in moderate lighting that makes its growth more manageable. It can look particularly effective when mixed with another carpeting species.

Pogostemon erectus

This beautiful stem plant tends to grow very straight upwards and has dense needle-like bright green leaves, giving it a very ornamental feel. It can be planted in the background, but I like to use it as a contrast between foreground and background plants due to its high-impact appearance. Stronger lighting will produce a larger diameter plant with shorter gaps between the leaves.

Background

Bacopa caroliniana

This is a classic stem plant suitable for beginners. It's a relatively slow grower with few demands and can easily be propagated by trimming and re-planting the off-cuts. As with all stem plants it looks best planted in groups and can form an attractive background in most aquariums.

Echinodorus "Bleherae"

Known in the hobby as the "Amazon sword," this rosette plant has been available for many decades. It is a very easy plant that will tolerate lower lighting and doesn't require CO_2 injection. A nutrient-rich substrate will definitely improve growth and any nutrient deficiencies are quickly shown via pale growth in new leaves.

Hygrophila "Siamensis 53B"

This is one of my favorite stem plants of all time because it is so easy and is suitable for almost any aquarium. It thrives in almost all conditions although it will show pale growth if starved of nutrients. Propagation is simple by trimming off excess growth and replanting. Suitable as a background plant for all size aquariums and perfect as a starter plant in new set-ups to help prevent algae.

Limnophila sessiflora

This is one of the easiest and fastest growing plants available in the hobby, making it perfect for beginners and as a helping plant for new set ups to help prevent algae. Its rapid growth will need trimming regularly. A great alternative to the popular *Cabomba* that requires stronger lighting.

Limnophila hippuroides

Similar to the more demanding *Limnophila aromatica*, this beautiful background stem plant will turn a magnificent red/purple color given sufficient lighting. It's an easy plant that will grow well without CO_2 injection but to see its full potential, strong lighting, CO_2 injection, and good nutrition are recommended. Responds very well to frequent trimming, sending out new shoots readily.

Ludwigia palustris

This red stem plant is a fast grower that will tolerate no CO_2 injection and lower lighting. However, to achieve a bright red color and compact growth, stronger lighting will be necessary. Excess growth can be trimmed and re-planting as required. It can be prone to producing aerial roots (roots that grow from the upper stems). These can be trimmed off if so desired.

Rotala rotundifolia

Rotala rotundifolia is a great background stem plant that's ideal for beginners due to its easy nature. It usually remains a green color in lower lighting levels but under intense light can turn an orange/red color. It's a fast grower that will respond well to frequent trimming to encourage new side shoots.

Vallisneria americana "Gigantea"

This classic aquarium plant species is hugely popular and commonly known as "Jungle val" amongst many hobbyists, especially in the US. It has the potential to grow extremely tall, making it suitable for background in larger aquascapes. It sends out runners in good growth conditions and can soon overtake the entire aquarium if left unchecked. *Vallisneria* is one of the few 100 percent submerged aquatic plant species that *only* grow under water (submerged).

Alternantheria reineckii "Pink"

This is a popular background stem plant that is widely recognizable due to its intense pink/red leaves and stems. Unlike many other aquarium plant species it is red even in its out-of-water (emerged) growth state, with most other species starting off green then turning red in appropriate aquarium conditions. Be aware that the Amano shrimp (*Caridina multidentata*) are known to enjoy eating its delicate leaves.

Rotala "Green"

Rotala "Green" is very similar to *Rotala rotundifolia* in its leave shape and size but slightly more demanding, doing best with CO_2 injection and moderate to high lighting. It remains a vibrant green color and rather than growing straight upwards, it can droop forward, adding an interesting effect to an aquascape. This "drooping" effect is more pronounced with higher light intensities.

Rotala wallichii

This delicate stem plant requires intense lighting and CO_2 injection to thrive but will reward you with beautiful dense red needle-like leaves. It does best in softer, more acidic water, but by using a soil substrate, achieving healthy growth is achievable with good lighting and nutrition.

EPIPHYTES AND MOSSES

Anubias barteri var. nana

This is one of the oldest aquarium plants made commonly available in the hobby. It is a very slow grower and does well in the shade where algae growth on the leaves is less likely. It should be attached to wood or rock with string or superglue, or by simply wedging it into a suitable gap where eventually the roots will self-attach.

Anubias "Petite"

Anubias "Petite" is very similar in demands to its larger cousins but has smaller leaves, making it suitable for nano aquariums. Large groups of this plant can also look stunning in bigger aquariums but can take many month to develop into a good size due to its slow growing nature. Good circulation and CO_2 injection will promote growth and help to prevent algae build-up on its leaves.

Bucephalandra "Wavy Green"

Bucephalandra species are relatively new in the aquascaping world but have quickly become very popular with many beautiful varieties now available. Unfortunately, their natural habitat in Borneo, Southeast Asia, is becoming increasingly decimated due to the monoculture of oil palm trees in order to produce palm oil. Treat it as you would *Anubias*.

Microsorum pteropus

The classic Java fern is one of my all-time favorite plants that can be grown in almost any aquarium. It doesn't require strong lighting or CO_2 injection, although as with all aquarium plants these will improve overall growth and condition. Due to its impactful size and shape *Microsorum* is ideal when used as a focal point plant attached to an appropriately located piece of wood or rock.

Microsorum pteropus "Trident"

Commonly known as "Trident" fern, this attractive *Microsorum* has a finer textured leaf formation consisting of three forks, hence the name. It is slightly more demanding than the regular Java fern so will definitely benefit from CO_2 injection and stronger lighting to get the best results. It is important to regularly remove any older dying leaves from the rhizome in order to keep it looking fresh and to maintain overall plant health.

Taxiphyllum barbieri

Also known as Java moss, this classic moss has been in the hobby for decades. It is undemanding of light and will grow in a wide range of aquarium conditions and nutrient levels. It is best attached to wood or rocks as thin layers of moss using thread or superglue. I prefer to add any mosses once the aquarium is mature with

a population of shrimp to help avoid algae build up in the moss.

Bolbitis heudelotii

Commonly known as the African water fern this beautiful epiphyte plant has interestingly shaped and bright green translucent leaves. It does best in areas with good circulation and will need CO_2 injection and moderate to high lighting levels to thrive. Given enough time it can grow very large and dominate an aquascape if not trimmed back. Thin out excess growth by sharply pulling away any unwanted leaves from the rhizome or simply cut back the rhizome and attached leaves as necessary.

Vesicularia dubyana "Christmas"

Christmas moss can be treated in a similar way to Java moss but it does best with moderate lighting and may need CO_2 injection to thrive. When viewed up close, the moss fronds grow in a Christmas tree–like pattern hence its name. Trim any excess moss back with sharp scissors and be aware that the off-cuts will sink so siphon these away as part of a water change.

Riccardia chamedryfolia

This is actually a liverwort and not a moss despite its appearance. Its compact growth gives it a great texture when attached to your hardscape. It's a slow grower and needs good lighting and CO_2 injection in order to look its best. It can take months to establish but looks beautiful if given the right conditions.

Floating

Salvinia auriculata

This small floating plant is a fast grower with small dangling roots. I like to add this to smaller aquariums at the start to help avoid algae issues. Because it's floating it is well-lit and has access to CO_2 in the air. This results in fast growth and plenty of oxygen production from the roots. Pale growth will indicate if more liquid fertilizer is required. Simply lift out excess growth with a net and dispose of carefully.

Limnobium laevigatum

Known as "Amazon frogbit," *Limnobium laevigatum* has a larger leaf than *Salvinia* with roots that can reach all the way to the bottom of the aquarium. For this reason, it's best used in larger aquariums although the dangling roots can look very effective in a more cryptic style aquascape where plenty of shade is desired. This can also promote some fish species breeding behavior.

Bulb

Nymphaea lotus

Also known as the "Tiger Lotus," this tropical lily originates from West Africa. It needs moderate to strong lighting without shade to grow well and a nutrient-rich substrate will improve long term health. Leaves that quickly grow to the aquarium surface can be trimmed back in order to keep the plant under control and to prevent excess overshadowing from floating leaves.

Aponogeton madagascariensis

This stunning plant is instantly recognizable with its unique leaf pattern giving it its common name, the "Madagascar lace plant." It does best with strong lighting, CO_2 injection and a nutrient-rich substrate. As with all bulb plants, the bulb should have its tip just above the substrate surface. If and when the leaves become too long simply trim the leaf next to the bulb to encourage new leaf growth.

APPENDIX III: AQUARIUM PLANT SPECIES LIST

Species Name	Type	Category
Alternanthera reineckii "Mini"	Stem	Medium
Alternanthera reineckii "Pink"	Stem	Medium
Alternanthera reineckii "Rosanvervig"	Stem	Medium
Anubias barteri var. barteri	Epiphyte	Easy
Anubias barteri var. caladiifolia	Epiphyte	Easy
Anubias barteri var. nana	Epiphyte	Easy
Anubias gracilis	Epiphyte	Easy
Anubias "Petite"	Epiphyte	Easy
Aponogeton boivinianus	Bulb	Medium
Aponogeton crispus	Bulb	Medium
Aponogeton longiplumulosus	Bulb	Medium
Aponogeton madagascariensis	Bulb	Medium
Aponogeton ulvaceus	Bulb	Medium
Bacopa australis	Stem	Medium
Bacopa caroliniana	Stem	Easy
Bacopa "Compact"	Stem	Easy
Bolbitis heudelotii	Epiphyte	Medium
Bucephalandra "Kedagang"	Epiphyte	Easy
Bucephalandra "Red"	Epiphyte	Easy
Bucephalandra "Wavy Green"	Epiphyte	Easy
Cabomba aquatica	Stem	Easy
Cardamine lyrate	Stem	Easy
Ceratophyllum demersum "Foxtail"	Floating	Easy
Ceratopsis thalictroides	Stem	Medium
Cladophora aegagropila	Algae ball	Easy

Crinum calamistratum	Bulb	Easy
Cryptocoryne albida "Brown"	Rosette	Easy
Cryptocoryne becketii "Petchii"	Rosette	Easy
Cryptocoryne crispatula	Rosette	Easy
Cryptocoryne parva	Rosette	Medium
Cryptocoryne undulata "Broad Leaves"	Rosette	Easy
Cryptocoryne undulata "Red"	Rosette	Easy
Cryptocoryne usteriana	Rosette	Easy
Cryptocoryne wendtii	Rosette	Easy
Cryptocoryne wendtii "Green"	Rosette	Easy
Cryptocoryne wendtii "Tropica"	Rosette	Easy
Cryptocoryne x willisii	Rosette	Easy
Cyperus helferi	Rosette	Medium
Echinodorus "Aquartica"	Rosette	Medium
Echinodorus "Barthii"	Rosette	Easy
Echinodorus "Bleherae"	Rosette	Easy
Echinodorus cordifolius "Fluitans"	Rosette	Easy
Echinodorus "Ozelot"	Rosette	Easy
Echinodorus "Ozelot Green"	Rosette	Easy
Echinodorus palaefolius	Rosette	Medium
Echinodorus "Red Diamond"	Rosette	Medium
Echinodorus "Reni"	Rosette	Easy
Echinodorus "Rosé"	Rosette	Easy
Egeria densa	Stem	Easy
Elatine hydropiper	Carpeting	Advanced
Eleocharis acicularis	Carpeting	Easy
Eleocharis acicularis "Mini"	Carpeting	Medium
Eleocharis montevidensis	Carpeting	Easy

Eleocharis parvula	Carpeting	Easy
Eriocaulon cinereum	Rosette	Advanced
Fissidens fontanus	Moss	Advanced
Glossostigma elatinoides	Carpeting	Advanced
Gratiola viscidula	Stem	Medium
Helanthium "Quadricostatus"	Carpeting	Easy
Helanthium tenellum "Green"	Carpeting	Easy
Helanthium "Vesuvius"	Rosette	Medium
Hemianthus callitrichoides	Carpeting	Advanced
Hemianthus micranthemoides	Stem	Advanced
Heteranthera zosterfolia	Stem	Easy
Hottonia palustris	Stem	Easy
Hydrocotyle tripartita	Carpeting	Medium
Hydrocotyle verticillata	Stem	Advanced
Hygrophila "Araguaia"	Stem	Medium
Hygrophila "Compact"	Stem	Easy
Hygrophila corymbosa	Stem	Easy
Hygrophila costata	Stem	Medium
Hygrophila difformis	Stem	Easy
Hygrophila pinnatifida	Stem	Medium
Hygrophila polysperma	Stem	Easy
Hygrophila polysperma "Rosanervig"	Stem	Easy
Hygrophila "Siamensis"	Stem	Easy
Hygrophila "Siamensis 53B"	Stem	Easy
Lagenandra meeboldii "Red"	Rosette	Easy
Lilaeopsis brasiliensis	Carpeting	Easy
Lilaeopsis mauritiana	Carpeting	Medium
Lilaeopsis novae-zelandiae	Carpeting	Easy

Limnobium laevigatum	Floating	Easy
Limnophila aquatica	Stem	Medium
Limnophila aromatica	Stem	Medium
Limnophila hippuridoides	Stem	Easy
Limnophila sessiflora	Stem	Easy
Lindernia rotundifolia	Stem	Easy
Littorella uniflora	Carpeting	Easy
Lobelia cardinalis	Stem	Easy
Ludwigia glandulosa	Stem	Medium
Ludwigia palustris	Stem	Easy
Ludwigia repens "Rubin"	Stem	Easy
Marsilea crenata	Carpeting	Medium
Marsilea hirsuta	Carpeting	Easy
Mayaca fluviatillis	Stem	Medium
Micranthemum "Monte Carlo"	Carpeting	Medium
Micranthemum umbrosum	Stem	Medium
Microsorum pteropus	Epiphyte	Easy
Microsorum pteropus "Narrow"	Epiphyte	Easy
Microsorum pteropus "Trident"	Epiphyte	Easy
Microsorum pteropus "Windeløv"	Epiphyte	Easy
Monosolenium tenerum	Moss	Easy
Murdannia keisak	Stem	Easy
Myriophyllum "Guyana"	Stem	Medium
Myriophyllum mattogrossense	Stem	Medium
Nesaea crassicaulis	Stem	Medium
Nymphaea lotus	Bulb	Medium
Nymphoides hydrophylla "Taiwan"	Bulb	Easy
Pogostemon erectus	Stem	Medium

Pogostemon helferi	Stem	Medium
Pogostemon stellata	Stem	Advanced
Ranunculus inundatus	Carpet	Medium
Riccardia chamedryfolia	Moss	Advanced
Riccia fluitans	Moss	Medium
Rotala "Bonsai"	Stem	Medium
Rotala "Green"	Stem	Medium
Rotala macrandra	Stem	Advanced
Rotala rotundifolia	Stem	Easy
Rotala "Vietnam H'ra"	Stem	Medium
Rotala wallichii	Stem	Advanced
Sagittaria subulata	Carpeting	Easy
Salvinia auriculata	Floating	Easy
Shinnersia rivularis "Weiss-Grün"	Stem	Medium
Staurogyne repens	Stem	Easy
Taxiphyllum Barbieri	Moss	Easy
Taxiphyllum "Flame"	Moss	Medium
Taxiphyllum "Spiky"	Moss	Easy
Taxiphyllum "Taiwan moss"	Moss	Easy
Utricularia graminifolia	Carpeting	Advanced
Vallisneria americana "Asiatica"	Rosette	Easy
Vallisneria americana "Gigantea"	Rosette	Easy
Vallisneria americana "Natans"	Rosette	Easy
Vallisneria nana	Rosette	Easy
Vallisneria spiralis "Tiger"	Rosette	Easy
Vesicularia dubyana "Christmas"	Moss	Medium
Vesicularia ferriei "Weeping"	Moss	Medium